D

Open Guides to Literature

Series Editor: Graham Martin (Professor of Literature,
The Open University)

Titles in the Series

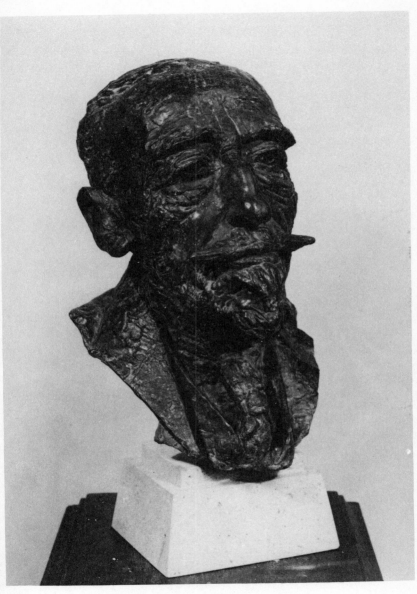

Bust of Joseph Conrad by Jacob Epstein
(Courtesy of National Portrait Gallery, London)

ANTHONY FOTHERGILL

Heart of Darkness

Open University Press
Milton Keynes · Philadelphia

Open University Press
12 Cofferidge Close
Stony Stratford
Milton Keynes MK11 1BY

and
1900 Frost Road, Suite 101
Bristol, PA 19007, USA

First Published 1989

British Library Cataloguing in Publication Data

Fothergill, Anthony
 Heart of Darkness. — (Open guides to literature)
 1. Fiction in English. Conrad, Joseph. Heart of
 Darkness — study outlines
 I. Title
 823'.912

 ISBN 0-335-15258-9
 ISBN 0-335-15257-0 (paper)

Library of Congress Cataloging-in-Publication Number Available

Typeset by Rowland Phototypesetting Limited
Bury St Edmunds, Suffolk
Printed in Great Britain by
J. W. Arrowsmith Limited, Bristol

Contents

Series Editor's Preface

The intention of this series is to provide short introductory books about major writers, texts, and literary concepts for students of courses in Higher Education which substantially or wholly involve the study of Literature.

The series adopts a pedagogic approach and style similar to that of Open University material for Literature courses. *Open Guides* aim to inculcate the reading 'skills' which many introductory books in the field tend, mistakenly, to assume that the reader already possesses. They are, in this sense, 'teacherly' texts, planned and written in a manner which will develop in the reader the confidence to undertake further independent study of the topic. They are 'open' in two senses. First, they offer a three-way tutorial exchange between the writer of the *Guide*, the text or texts in question, and the reader. They invite readers to join in an exploratory discussion of texts, concentrating on their key aspects and on the main problems which readers, coming to the texts for the first time, are likely to encounter. The flow of a *Guide* 'discourse' is established by putting questions for the reader to follow up in a tentative and searching spirit, guided by the writer's comments, but not dominated by an over-arching and single-mindedly-pursued argument or evaluation, which itself requires to be 'read'.

Guides are also 'open' in a second sense. They assume that literary texts are 'plural', that there is no end to interpretation, and that it is for the reader to undertake the pleasurable task of discovering meaning and value in such texts. *Guides* seek to provide, in compact form, such relevant biographical, historical and cultural information as bears upon the reading of the text, and they point the reader to a selection of the best available critical discussions of it. They are not in themselves concerned to propose, or to counter, particular readings of the texts, but rather to put *Guide* readers in a position to do that for themselves. Experienced travellers learn to dispense with guides, and so it should be for readers of this series.

This *Open Guide* will be best studied in conjunction with the Penguin English Library edition of the text, with an introduction by Paul O'Prey (1983). All page references are to this edition.

Graham Martin

Acknowledgements

My thanks go first to Graham Martin, who has shown formidable patience and attention during the preparation of this book. From its earliest stages he offered wonderfully appropriate and worried advice. Some of the thoughts in the book are of such longevity that I cannot trace accurately my full indebtedness to those I know have contributed to them, but Peter Faulkner, Ron Tamplin and Richard Maltby can share part of the blame. Ideas in the book, especially in Chapter 5, have been tried out at the School of English 'Theory and Text' Seminars, Exeter University. But it is not just for his inspiring and hosting of those meetings that I would like to thank Michael Wood. He has shared a way of thinking, generous and subtle, that cannot be calculated in pages.

Charlie Page, whose ideas and comments often seem wisely and widely tangential and always prove central, will sensibly fail to find anything remotely reminiscent of his own thoughts here.

Finally, I would like to thank Karen Edwards. From her I have received so much energy, help and argument at every stage of the writing, that it seems quite churlish to absolve her with the generically customary clause that I alone am responsible for the final work, its mistakes and limitations. It wouldn't have been, without her.

I would like to dedicate the book to Ron and Leni Fothergill, for waiting so patiently.

11 March 1989
Exeter

1. Meanings and Readings

Every story, even the simplest, seems to call for interpretation. Kafka tells the following parable:

> Leopards break into the temple and drink to the dregs what is in the sacrificial pitchers; this is repeated over and over again; finally it can be calculated in advance, and it becomes a part of the ceremony.[1]

Is it a story about the taming of the dangerous, about the incorporating of a threat into a familiar routine? Is it about the intelligent sophistication and power of human culture over primal animal needs? Or does it concern the ability of society to assess, contain, and control troublesome opposition and 'otherness'? Is it about the savage origins of civilized behaviour and ritual? Or is it . . . ? We can't let the story rest. What does it 'really mean'? In its troubling simplicity, it seems to demand translation into other terms. It calls for a meaning or meanings which it nevertheless then resists for their reductiveness.

A further reading: the parable is about the process of reading itself. We are not content to let strange experiences, the foreign animals of our imagination, simply intrude into our daily lives. Once they have entered, we feel the need to absorb and assimilate them to the familiar by giving them 'a meaning' in familiar (and therefore less disturbingly potent) terms. We are not content, that is, with 'just reading', just letting the foreign 'otherness' of a work have its way with us. Rather, in reading the work we find its mystery creates in us an appetite to discover '*the* meaning' — as if the appetite, once whetted, could ever be anything but temporarily satisfied.

And yet our urgency to translate the experience of a story into a meaning is sometimes matched only by the need of the storyteller to impart one, as if in the moment of dying, the teller's life were flashing before him and he alone could offer up to others the summary wisdom of his insights into it.

Marlow is such a storyteller in *Heart of Darkness*. Though ostensibly his tale is that of another's, Kurtz's, death, it is as much an account of his, Marlow's, 'culminating point of experience'. The weight and determination of his narrative convinces us of the centrality of this experience – even if, or perhaps because, we feel his need to tell his story may exceed his fictional listeners' willingness to attend to it. The telling of his story seems as important as the death he tells of. But just as we have found with Kafka's parable, Marlow is acutely conscious that the meaning of his experience is neither stable nor easily transmissible. At one point, he interrupts the story of his journey up river to find and rescue Kurtz to comment to his listeners aboard the *Nellie*:

> 'He [Kurtz] was just a word for me. I did not see the man in the name any more than you do. Do you see him? Do you see the story? Do you see anything? It seems to me I am trying to tell you a dream – making a vain attempt, because no relation of a dream can convey the dream-sensation, that commingling of absurdity, surprise, and bewilderment in a tremor of struggling revolt, that notion of being captured by the incredible which is of the very essence of dreams . . .'
> He was silent for a while.
> '. . . No, it is impossible; it is impossible to convey the life-sensation of any given epoch of one's existence – that which makes its truth, its meaning – its subtle and penetrating essence. It is impossible. We live, as we dream – alone . . .'   (p. 57)

It is an important passage, one to which we will have to return, in which the narrator self-consciously draws attention to his own activity, the difficult task of narrating meaning. Does the difficulty lie in conveying the experience to others, or in the very 'unknowable-ness' of its meaning? The emphasis here seems to be on the former. But as the narration proceeds, we begin to doubt whether there is a meaning, a reducible core of truth rendered up in the telling. With its incidents redolent of the absurd or enigmatic, the story is pervaded by an atmosphere of the mysterious and incomprehensible. This generates the need for interpretations (on Marlow's part, on the reader's part) but never fully seems to offer settled ones: the meaning is constantly deferred, delayed. Is it ever finally disclosed? Phrases which echo through the whole work – 'dim suspicion', 'ominous', 'brooding gloom', 'inscrutable intention' (and there are many more) – promise and postpone a resolving signification.

Let us take as example the title of Conrad's tale. It seems simple enough: *Heart of Darkness*. What do we think it means? To what does it refer and with what tone and significance? We are used to novels whose titles, referentially clear, begin to offer a focus for our reading: *Mansfield Park*, *Tess of the D'Urbervilles*, *A Passage to*

India. At the outset we think we know roughly where we are, even if these titles ultimately reveal themselves to be more problematic than we thought. But *Heart of Darkness*?

We need only imagine adding a couple of definite or indefinite articles to the title – and then taking them away again – to realize the ambiguity of its reference and qualification. Has 'Darkness' an adjectival or nominative function? Does 'Heart' qualify 'Darkness' or vice versa? Does it mean 'the centre of darkness' or 'the heart which is dark'? Both possibilities are open to us, surely. Conrad altered the title from its original magazine version, *The Heart of Darkness*. Doesn't this indicate an intentional opening up of ambiguity? At one stroke the inwardness of the individual human heart is equated with the massive exteriority of place. The very title seems to encapsulate a 'modernist' moment in its tensions and ambivalences. Think of Picasso's bull's head/bicycle handle-bars and saddle, or Schoenberg's relying on tonality to subvert it. Like a verbal version of those black and white images used in tests of visual perception (is it a white vase on a black ground or two black faces in silhouette; a wizened old woman or a beautiful young one?), the title confronts us with language which won't, as it were, stand still. So we can take it for a procedure of central importance that Conrad adopts at all levels of his writing: he creates systems of signification and reference that are radically unstable.

As our reading progresses, the title retrospectively accumulates further and ambiguous connotations. As Marlow starts his account of his journey to rescue Kurtz, the 'darkness' seems to stand for the goal of that journey. But, we gradually begin to wonder, does this centre of darkness have geographical, metaphysical, or psychological significance? The words grow in resonance and ambiguity. 'Heart', we see, can come to be associated with centre, originating core, soul, and love, but also with the seat of monstrous passions, irrationality, and even hollowness; and 'darkness' comes to connote the unknown, the evil, and the savage, but also the elemental, the vital, the uncontaminated.

Given this radically ambivalent language, it is not surprising that Conrad's tale has generated a massive, indeed exhausting, body of critical commentary. But notice that there is something paradoxical about such critical enterprises. In their range these interpretative readings testify to the quality of plurality and multivalency that *Heart of Darkness* embodies; in their specific contributions they seek to offer a graspable but therefore reduced context for meaning. This may be the inevitable fate of criticism. To see something critically, after all, is to propose a context for understanding it. But this context or frame, which orders and refines, also excludes: how can it avoid a premature closing down of the play of meaning? The contextualizing frame offered by a formal or political or mythical or psychological critical reading promises at once coherence and closure.

There is a paradox here. The readerly desire to arrest the play of multiple meanings by settling on a 'closed' one characteristically takes as its object works whose 'classic' quality lies precisely in their demonstrable capacity to engender a variety of readings in the historical course of their reception. *Heart of Darkness* is not alone in being a work which powerfully exhibits multivalency of meaning. Is it possible that it has become a seminal work in the twentieth century precisely because of this paradox? It seems to answer the felt need for works both to exemplify a broader cultural preoccupation with the relativity of 'truth', with scepticism, and ambiguity, and yet to entice with the dangled hope of an end to all that.

The critic of *Heart of Darkness* is in a particularly teasing predicament. As we will find, the work's texture and strategies problematize closure, that is, a resolving kernel of meaning. The reader/critic acknowledges this – and then goes on to provide one. (Can we escape this paradox?) Perhaps we are all sympathetic to the 'framing narrator' – the anonymous speaker who introduces us to Marlow on board the *Nellie* – when he says almost nostalgically, 'The yarns of seamen have a direct simplicity, the whole meaning of which lies within the shell of a cracked nut' (p. 30).

I will later be asking you to consider the use Conrad makes of the framing narrator and his relationship to Marlow's story as a way of investigating the question of our relationship to the narrative of *Heart of Darkness*. For the moment let me suggest that critical readings, however 'pluralist' in intention, have tended to fall into four categories (which can be seen as variations of rendering the title of the work): they are, roughly, political, cultural, psychological, or mythical.

The first would see the 'heart of darkness' as having primarily geographical reference. The work then becomes an account of a journey up the Congo into 'darkest' Africa, although – and we will need to ask why – these proper names are never given us. Marlow's story then becomes a vehicle for Conrad to mount a critique of European colonialism with its imperialistic impulses towards profit, exploitation, and destruction. A second reading, historical but super-ficially less political, relies on a context offered by late nineteenth-century anthropological views on 'the savage' and 'the civilized,' on evolution and the origins of civilization. According to this view, Marlow's comments on the barbarity and brutal instincts he dis-covers in the darkness suggest a model for a kind of 'archeology of civilization'. Conrad's work then becomes a critique of complacent

Victorian ideas of civilized progress, the journey into the interior exposing the savage and primitive which lie beneath the civilized veneer of European culture. A third kind of interpretation sees the darkness as a psychological space of the unconscious self, which Marlow, on a journey of psycho-sexual initiation, comes glimpsingly to perceive. A fourth, finding endorsement in Conrad's own comments on the symbolic meaning of his writing, translates the 'darkness' into a metaphysical, mythical, or religious category. Marlow's journey may then be seen as a mythological descent into the underworld, a spiritual ascent to transcendental knowledge, or an ethical struggle of moral good and evil.

As with any work which generates such a multiplicity of readings, we will have to ask whether we are dealing with competing and mutually exclusive interpretations or whether we can more profitably look at them as a series of transformations of the same text. My purpose at present is twofold. First, as you start to read the novel, I want to draw preliminary attention to these interpretations as possible 'routes' others have taken into it. We will have the opportunity of assessing the merits of them later. Secondly, but more importantly, I would distinguish the aim of the present Guide from them. Rather than positing here a further 'better' thematic interpretation, I want to emphasize the processes of reading. As we shall see, *Heart of Darkness* does provide material for these thematic interpretations, but more profoundly, it offers excellent ground for us to become self-conscious about the activity of reading. The aim is to become simultaneously a naïve and sophisticated reader, naïvely enjoying the story as it unravels and self-consciously becoming aware of what we are doing when we are reading — and enjoying that, too.

I am stressing reading here, as I will throughout the Guide, to highlight immediately an aspect of *Heart of Darkness* which I take to be central and which I want you to pursue. Over and above our examining and adjudicating between specific readings of *Heart of Darkness*, I want to focus on how the novel above all else foregrounds the activity of 'reading' itself, which we should define at its broadest: not just our readings of Marlow, or Marlow's (and others') readings of Kurtz, the jungle, history, colonial practices, but the sheer inescapability of the fact of reading — even when we think we are 'just looking'. Reading and the attributing of meaning is, it seems, along with eating and sleeping, one of the conditions of being human.

This may sound like pulling up the plant to check that its roots are growing, but unlike growing plants, the self-conscious reading of books does not kill the books; rather, it enriches our understanding of them and of ourselves. This self-awareness can enlighten us not just on the merits of a particular interpretation but on the ways in which *what* we choose to concentrate on in the work and the *kinds* of questions we raise are determined by and generate the reading we want.

One of my presuppositions is that *Heart of Darkness*, in this respect so characteristic of other Modernist narratives,[2] demands the kind of close (but not closed) attention to its detailed texture that we may be more used to giving when we read and discuss poetry. This is not just because the symbolic 'thickness' of Conrad's language reinforces the sense of 'the poetic'. He also makes rich and fertile use of various narrative and stylistic devices – ambiguity, as we have seen, but also narrative and linguistic repetition, inversions, parallelisms, paradox, allusion, and elaborate image constellations. And these devices make for a narrative density which can really best be penetrated only by a close and remembering reading such as we give to the lyric poem.

It is odd how readily metaphors used to describe critical practice – 'density', 'getting to the heart of', 'penetrating to the core', 'casting light on' – mimic many of the gestures we 'discover' in Conrad's story itself. We mimic Marlow as we journey through the story seeking to unravel the yarn. But this mimicking works both ways. In so many of the detailed incidents, Marlow's experience, too, is that of a reader/listener. He is a persistent reader (and mis-reader) of signs and appearances. He is offered accounts (readings) of characters and activities (of Kurtz, of Company practices) which he has to evaluate. And like us he waits expectantly for 'the voice' which will sum up his narrative experience.

I will elaborate upon this subsequently, but presently suffice it to say that – as with any critical text – we should try to be as aware as possible of our own (and others') critical procedures as we go along. And this implies that while this essay may take the form of proposing 'key issues', our reading of the tale may make even these 'keys' increasingly problematic: as if, presumed by this metaphor, there *were* keys to unlock the casket for meaning.

One such 'key' (to embrace the contradiction immediately) is often thought to be the biographical connection between the author and his work. In the case of *Heart of Darkness* we know of Conrad's own journey up the Congo in 1890 some nine years previous to the tale's publication. That fact seems to invite comparison of the two spheres, the literary and the 'real' (a 'real' which, of course, we only have access to through other, usually written, accounts). Conrad himself gave credence to the biographical reading of literature:

> I know that a novelist lives in his work. He stands there, the only
> reality in an invented world, amongst imaginary things, happenings

and people. Writing about them, he is only writing about himself. Every novel contains an element of autobiography – and this can hardly be denied, since the creator can only explain himself in his creations.[3]

But the issue is a complex one. Recently, critics have argued the appropriateness or otherwise of relating the work to the author's biography and debated the relevance of authorial commentary. Some hold that such sources provide a significant historical context for a fuller understanding of the text – unless you regard the work as so completely autonomous from all social and historical determinants that there are no contexts. Others alert us to the danger of seeing the created work simply as a direct reflection of prior, originating experience in the 'real' world, and the fallacy of regarding the author as the fully conscious producer and controller of the work's meaning. A further question is whether such contextual knowledge best precedes or supplements a first reading of the work.

My own view is that while we should not privilege the writer as the interpreting authority, nor naïvely assume the truth-status of biography, the work *has* a historical (personal, social, and cultural) specificity, knowledge of which can only aid our understanding. So the following paragraphs will offer brief remarks pertaining to the biographical context. However, that said, as a chief aim of the Guide is to highlight processes of reading, and as you can only have a first reading once, you may like to turn to that 'opening' reading at once, before perusing the biographical summary which follows.

Biography of a Double Man

In 1924, the last year of Conrad's life, Jacob Epstein, a fellow Polish emigré, executed a sculpture of him which, despite his rapidly declining health and volatile nervous state, captures well a characteristic impression of fortitude – and also of doubleness – in Conrad.

'Homo duplex', Conrad once called himself, adding wittily that in his case it 'had more than one meaning'.[4] Duplicity? We are faced once more with the difficulties of interpretation and proliferation of meanings. The sculpture certainly reads in at least two ways. A respectable, fastidiously cravated and groomed elderly gentleman, self-assured and self-contained, can also be seen as a weathered and solitary individual confronting an unpleasant and immensely demanding fate. The pose and surface texture suggest grace under pressure. Though Conrad was by this time the most famous living English novelist, Epstein's Conrad is not simply looking inward upon his own achievement, but definitely outward towards . . . he knows not what. A double view or position – or displacement, which comes to the same thing – provides a useful key to an understanding of Conrad's life and to the ambivalences and contradictions of his work, which will be a recurring theme of this guide. Conrad never inhabited clear, stable positions. The effects of this can be seen everywhere: from his double nationality, the two professional careers he pursued, and his mixed social/class identity – to the destabilizing, double view of the ironies in his writing.

An aristocratic figure from an ancient Polish noble family, in his final year he declined the public accolade of a knighthood from his adopted country – and did so in a letter recalling proudly his association in 'hard toil and unforgotten friendships with British Working men'[5] – as if, unlike British aristocrats, he placed more value in the earned acknowledgement among equals of personal effort and achievement, than in public, institutional, or hereditary respectability. Marlow's admiration for conscientious work over social appearances may here find an echo.

The hard work had been in the merchant navy, in which he made his first career, initially in France, then in Britain. But just when he had climbed, via Able Seaman and Second Mate, to the pinnacle of Master Mariner, he abandoned that career, twenty years into its making, for that of a sedentary, but for him no less arduous, profession as creative writer. And even at that peak, as the elder statesman of English letters, he still spoke English – his third language – with a heavy Polish accent and a liberal scattering of French.

He was born in 1857, in a Poland partitioned and occupied since 1795 by Russia, Prussia, and Austria. The tyrannical colonization of central and eastern Poland by Russia never extinguished Polish nationalist fervour nor the insurrectionary movements it spawned, active in which was Conrad's father, Apollo Korzeniowski. That meant that for Józef Teodor Konrad Nałęcz Korzeniowski, as he was christened (and as occasionally throughout his life he continued to sign himself), there was not a comfortable and settled upper-class existence, but an early upbringing within a fervently patriotic and therefore revolutionary household. This conjunction of aristocracy with radicalism was, however paradoxical, profound. Apollo Korzeniowski was a national political figure (and translator of Shakespeare, Dickens, and Hugo) whose socialist 'subversive' political activities led him and his family into forced exile in Russia and to his and his wife's early deaths. For Conrad, then, the experience of being colonized – politically and economically tyrannized – was something which came to him early. Exile and solitariness were also almost 'inborn'. From 1869, now orphaned, he was brought up, back in Poland, by his uncle Tadeusz Bobrowski, whom in 1874 Conrad persuaded to let him depart for Marseilles – fulfilling a childhood passion to go to sea. His social and cultural background in Poland had provided him with French, whose literature, along with English in translation, he had been 'fed on' in his youth. Travel books, adventure stories, Hugo, Marryat, Cooper, had fed his boyhood imagination. Later it was to be Flaubert, Maupassant and Turgenev. But the Polish upper classes saw the French connection as cultural: they didn't envisage the merchant navy.

So a further, social, dislocation brought Conrad into the variously dangerous, romantic, arduous, and boring world of the merchant navy. For four years he voyaged in French merchant ships around the Mediterranean, to Martinique and the West Indies, training as a mariner. In 1878 he joined an English ship, first plying the east coast, with later ocean runs to the Far East and Australia. Learning English was one requirement for his Master Mariner qualification, which he achieved in 1886, the same year that he became a naturalized British subject, partly for career reasons, partly to declare a liberation from his native country's oppressor, Russia.

His career as a seaman was not untroubled. His appointments often ended abruptly because of quarrels with his superiors – a tension which registers in Marlow's attitude to his employers. But it did put him in immediate and prolonged contact with men from a class and background quite alien to his, but in whom he learnt to recognize the values of a simple and unproblematic devotion to demanding, monotonous, dangerous work. 'Work', as we will see, is a powerful theme in the novel. How it is evaluated is crucial.

His voyages to India, the Far East, and Australia naturally involved him in personal encounters and locations[6] on which he was later to draw extensively for material for his fiction, from his earliest works, *Almayer's Folly* (1895) and *Lord Jim* (1900), to 'The Secret Sharer' (1910), to *The Shadow-Line* (1916) and *The Rescue* (1920).

One of those commissions, Conrad's engagement in 1890 with the Société Anonyme Belge pour le Commerce du Haut-Congo, took him to the Congo. After months looking for employment, his position was secured largely through the good offices of Marguerite Poradowska, not his 'aunt' but a widow of a second cousin. Their extensive correspondence reveals how important a role she, a novelist herself, played in Conrad's life, particularly in encouraging him to pursue his early literary interests. As a 'parallel' to Marlow's aunt, she provides an interesting if contrasting focus in our consideration of his view of women.

Conrad's assignment with the Société Anonyme was to replace on the steamboat *Florida* a Danish Captain Freiesleben, who had been murdered after a quarrel with tribesmen. Conrad's Africa journey to Stanley Falls is recorded in his *Congo Diary*, which bears

witness to his direct exposure to the brutalities of the colonial
scramble: 'Saw at a camp-place the dead body of a Backongo. Shot?
Horrid smell . . .'.[7] The cruelty Marlow depicts is not merely imagined. How he presents it, though, and to what narrative and
politically critical end, remains for us to consider.

Feverish sickness and near mental breakdown were one result of the
horrors Conrad experienced in the Congo. Months of recuperation,
followed by further difficulties in getting the kind of postings he
wished for, frustrated his career hopes. But meanwhile the critical
success of his first novel, *Almayer's Folly*, and a modest inheritance
from his uncle Tadeusz encouraged him to abandon the sea – though
not the experiences he had gained there – and embark on his second
profession.

   That profession saw Conrad's contribution of some of the
major writing of the century. From *The Nigger of the 'Narcissus'*
(1897) and *Lord Jim* (1900), by way of *Nostromo* (1904), *The Secret
Agent* (1907), and *Under Western Eyes* (1911), to *Victory* (1915),
The Rescue (1920), and *The Rover* (1923), Conrad worked on and
out of a society and literary culture which called for a radical
reassessment and reinvigoration. To that demand, by the time of
his death in 1924, Conrad had massively answered. *Heart of
Darkness* was an early and an abidingly powerful testimony to this
achievement.

   There is a general point I would draw from this. Conrad's
'doubleness' caused him to straddle boundaries. But though dis-
locating and unstable, this half-adopted, half-forced position of
marginality provided him, I would suggest, with a critical edge, the
perspective of someone inside-and-yet-outside. Politically, cultur-
ally, socially – and not least, as a writer, linguistically – this
marginality forced him into a kind of searching self-consciousness.
To be able to register nuances, contradictions, oppositions in all the
things a culture takes for granted – this is the benefit of never being
quite 'one of us'. Conrad's doubleness, then, was the precondition
perhaps of his profound critique.

**If you haven't yet started, read the opening pages of *Heart of
Darkness* now.** In the following chapter I will concentrate on the
early pages of the novel (pp. 27–32), scrutinizing the ways in which
they invite us to exercise our readerly expectations, self-consciously
investigating how the work confirms, elaborates, or confounds them.
The chapter will not so much resolve questions as raise them, to offer
provisional thematic 'hooks' on which to hang our thoughts in our
subsequent reading.

2. Stories and Histories

(i) Framing Expectations

I have referred so far to Marlow's story – which is probably how we think about *Heart of Darkness*. But there's a sense in which the novel offers us, like a set of Russian dolls, a series of stories, one embedded within the other. How many stories are there? First, there is the framing narrator's, to which I have already referred. On board the *Nellie* on the Thames, it is he who introduces us to Marlow and formally closes the narrative. As if within imaginary brackets, everything else – including Marlow's narration – is contained within this frame. We will soon be attending to the implications of this structural feature of the novel, for it immediately provokes questions. Why not just have Marlow tell the story directly? Why 'enclose' it like this? What role does this narrator play? As it is, we are asked to accept that this anonymous narrator (with a remarkable facility for recall!) can repeat verbatim Marlow's story of his journey to Kurtz, the second story in the series. And Marlow's encloses yet another, Kurtz's story of his exploits in the interior.

Story within story within story. And as if these stories were not enough, we will discover other ones as we read on, all of them, like Marlow's journey itself, bearing in upon Kurtz. There's the self-contained mini-story about Fresleven (with troubling parallels to Kurtz) and also others which we might call proto-narratives: other people's versions of Kurtz and his 'achievements'. The Manager of the Central Station, the Russian Harlequin, and, on Marlow's return to Europe, the Company representative, the 'cousin', the journalist, and the Intended – all these offer Marlow (and us) their skeletal stories of Kurtz. However sketchy they may be, they provide, at least potentially, readings of Kurtz that compete with Marlow's, and all of them contest the ground of narration which constitutes the novel.

Reading the novel for the first time, of course, we only gradually recognize this 'embedding' device. We thus come to the work trying

to orientate ourselves primarily to the first-person anonymous narrator, for we are likely to assume (for want of knowing any better at
the outset) that he will be telling of *his* experiences. To see how this
negotiation with the text commences, let us first look at the crucial
opening pages – crucial because they do open the book and our
critical attention is focused on them as we seek to gain firm bearings
within the novel; crucial also because very soon a radical shift of
focus (from framing narrator to Marlow) undermines any tentative
security of position we might feel we have achieved. Apart from our
assimilating information about setting and character, what significance do we draw in these first pages from the *way* we are implicitly
addressed by the first-person narrator?

Consider these opening remarks:

> The Director of Companies was our captain and our host. We four
> affectionately watched his back as he stood in the bows looking to
> seaward. On the whole river there was nothing that looked half so
> nautical. He resembled a pilot, which to a seaman is trustworthiness
> personified. It was difficult to realize his work was not out there in the
> luminous estuary, but behind him within the brooding gloom.
> Between us there was, as I have already said somewhere, the bond of
> the sea. Besides holding our hearts together through long periods of
> separation, it had the effect of making us tolerant of each other's yarns
> – and even convictions. The Lawyer – the best of old fellows – had,
> because of his many years and many virtues, the only cushion on deck,
> and was lying on the only rug. The Accountant had brought out
> already a box of dominoes, and was toying architecturally with the
> bones. Marlow sat cross-legged right aft, leaning against the mizzen-
> mast. He had sunken cheeks, a yellow complexion, a straight back, an
> ascetic aspect, and, with his arms dropped, the palms of hands
> outwards, resembled an idol. The Director, satisfied the anchor had
> good hold, made his way aft and sat down amongst us. We exchanged
> a few words lazily. Afterwards there was silence on board the
> yacht.   (pp. 27–8)

**As you read this for the first time, what sort of story do you expect?
What tone does the narrator adopt towards his colleagues and his
(assumed) listeners/readers? What does he assume that you know? Is
Marlow treated like the rest?**

DISCUSSION

The first thing that struck me was the tone of familiarity – both of the
men for one another ('We four affectionately watched his back') and,
somehow in parallel, of the narrator for the implied reader. The
primary function of the passage, it seems, is to convey the factual
information (who is on board, the setting); the established sense
of familiarity appears merely a secondary effect. But equally striking

is the way that the narrator makes us complicit in his assumptions. He is narrating as if he has the relationship with us that a story-teller has with a familiar audience gathered around him. The notional addressees of the narrator, the implied listeners, 'know' the narrator – 'as I have said somewhere before' – and are familiar, if not in fact with the specific individuals (though in the easy reference by name to Marlow even that is suggested), at least with the type of the Director of Companies, the Lawyer, the Accountant. And although as actual readers sitting in the isolation of our own rooms, we are not identical to the implied addressees, the rhetoric of this opening passage invites us to assent to the shared knowledge, values, and assumptions of this 'familiar' metropolitan community. Whatever our gender, we acknowledge male solidarity, mutual respect among working professionals, and the sense of confirmed social place. Overall, there is something 'clubby' in the tone, which leads me to anticipate the sort of adventure story that would be savoured by such men as the narrator introduces.

Second, Marlow. He is named. Why, I wonder, aren't the others? He is given a fuller description, which sets him slightly apart from the others. Is this a narrative tactic, simply to signify a homing-in for concentration on one character who'll prove more central than the others? Or does this identification also register his real difference from them? **Look at the description of Marlow. What do you make of the motif of him as an ascetic idol, sitting in a buddha-like pose? Why is the word 'idol' used? What connotations does it carry, particularly coming after the reference to 'bones'?**

DISCUSSION

The language of the text in its detail seems to me to be sending out contradictory meanings. The buddha-like pose implies that Marlow will resemble a voice of wisdom, a semi-divine figure worthy perhaps of veneration. But there is something troubling, too, about 'idol'. It evokes the idea of false and graven images. This ambivalence of meaning is carried over into the description of the day's end, with its 'exquisite brilliance' but also its 'brooding gloom'. So on the one hand the narrator sounds confident and familiar, but on the other, troubling ambivalences creep into his words. We cannot, nor need we feel we must, resolve these meanings harmoniously at the outset. The uncertainty of judgement which this disturbance provokes is part of the process of orientation by which we approach the text.

By 'orientation' I mean the largely unconscious give and take, the processes of assimilation of information, ordering, judgement, and imaginative reconstruction, and all the other delicate forms of

readerly activity by which we negotiate the text. It is as if we are in
dialogue with the text, with another voice. We are one half of a
conversation (unspeaking but by no means passive) through which
its material, language, comes to meaning. We come to adjudge the
tone, the assertions, and the assumptions of this other voice, construe
them, and establish expectations on the basis of them.[1]

'Orientation' is not a once-only affair. The text is constantly
making us reassess our judgements and our position as readers. But
one point to remember (and in this Conrad's is no different from any
other work): even in an initial reading the process is not one of first
reading, then of a more conscious assessing, speculating about,
projecting on this work, activating our knowledge of other reading
to contextualize it. Rather, all these processes go on from the start,
and indeed it is these activities which constitute 'reading'.

(ii) Views of the Thames, Views of History

Let us turn to the passage taking us up to the point of Marlow's
narration. It both describes the Thames at sunset and conveys the
silent meditation of the framing narrator, which retards the flow of
explicit narrative action. We may easily read over it as 'mere
description', 'atmosphere'. But it is often just such passages whose
charged rhetorical assurance establishes for the reader expectational
norms.

> Forthwith a change came over the waters, and the serenity became less
> brilliant but more profound. The old river in its broad reach rested
> unruffled at the decline of day, after ages of good service done to the
> race that peopled its banks, spread out in the tranquil dignity of a
> waterway leading to the uttermost ends of the earth. We looked at the
> venerable stream not in the vivid flush of a short day that comes and
> departs for ever, but in the august light of abiding memories. And
> indeed nothing is easier for a man who has, as the phrase goes,
> 'followed the sea' with reverence and affection, than to evoke the great
> spirit of the past upon the lower reaches of the Thames. The tidal
> current runs to and fro in its unceasing service, crowded with mem-
> ories of men and ships it had borne to the rest of home or to the battles
> of the sea. It had known and served all the men of whom the nation is
> proud, from Sir Francis Drake to Sir John Franklin, knights all, titled
> and untitled – the great knights-errant of the sea. It had borne all the
> ships whose names are like jewels flashing in the night of time, from
> the *Golden Hind* returning with her round flanks full of treasure, to be
> visited by the Queen's Highness and thus pass out of the gigantic tale,
> to the *Erebus* and *Terror*, bound on other conquests – and that never
> returned. It had known the ships and the men. They had sailed from
> Deptford, from Greenwich, from Erith – the adventurers and the
> settlers; kings' ships and the ships of men on 'Change; captains,

admirals, the dark 'interlopers' of Eastern trade, and the com-
missioned 'generals' of East India fleets. Hunters for gold or pursuers
of fame, they all had gone out on that stream, bearing the sword, and
often the torch, messengers of the might within the land, bearers of a
spark from the sacred fire. What greatness had not floated on the ebb
of that river into the mystery of an unknown earth! . . . The dreams of
men, the seed of commonwealths, the germs of empires.   (pp. 28–9)

Look at such phrases as 'unceasing service', 'tranquil dignity',
'venerable stream'. **What attitude towards the Thames and its
history is implied by the narrator? What sense of history and
historical action do the references to Sir Francis Drake and Sir John
Franklin evoke for you? Finally, what sort of tale do you imagine this
passage to be introducing, bearing in mind the men it refers to as
'knights-errant'?**

DISCUSSION

The narrative voice, it seems to me, is consciously rhetorical,
measured, and confident – and this reflects its subject, a national
history. A whole network of language – 'venerable', 'dignified',
'unceasing service', 'august', 'reverence' – reinforces the implicit
assertion of the description and offers a particular view of history.
For the narrator, history is heroic, progressive, incontrovertible. The
allusions (to Sir John Franklin, to Sir Francis Drake and the *Golden
Hind*) also imply a certain sort of reader, one whose competence
enables the correct decoding of the historical referents and more
importantly one who endorses the positive judgements made on
these 'heroic' figures. But you may say at this point, 'I don't know
who Sir John Franklin is, nor anything about him! So I can't know
that the narrator means that yet another heroic act was the fatal trip
of the *Erebus* under Franklin's captaincy in search of the North West
Passage in 1845'. True. But competence is something a text both
assumes and can create. The words, 'Sir John Franklin' or '*Erebus*',
function in their context as a sign that I translate as 'heroic historical
figure' or 'momentous event in my national history' (without my
consciously questioning the implications of these terms). History as
chronological time becomes narratable as 'the gigantic tale' of acts of
nobility and renown. These historical acts are rhetorically rendered
as adventures, conquests, exploration, commercial and military
exploits. I almost said 'exploitation', but within the terms of the
rhetoric and ideology which it articulates, that word would not be
possible. It would tend to subvert the ostensible beliefs. And yet there
is a disturbing undercurrent just observable in the very balance and
rhythms of sentences which push towards an affirmation of this
historical view. Look at the phrases, 'dark interlopers' and bearers of

'the sword and often the torch'. **Are these unambivalently positive? Is the narrator quietly modifying his view of history as a glorious tale? Put another way, is he deliberately punning when he talks of 'knights-errant' and 'the germs of Empires'?**

DISCUSSION

In brief, my answer to each of these questions would be 'no'. But I'm aware that this reading leaves me with a profoundly ambivalent text whose language – but not the conscious narrator – looks both ways, lying and revealing truths simultaneously. In my reading, 'interlopers' and bearers of the sword and torch (of knowledge, or the fires of destruction?) smack potentially of violence, illegality, and brute force. But they rub shoulders with heroic captains, royal servants, and bearers of a sacred spark. The affirmed 'greatness' covers heroism – but also those negatives of mendacity, violence, and might. The rhetorical sweep of the phrases (note their balance and assonance) culminates in a final affirmative exclamation. But it brings the negatives in its wake. The narrator's confident eloquence overrides the hesitation necessary to ponder the phrases' full implications. But the implications are there. It is as if the language speaks more than the narrator could possibly explicitly say. That is why he is still able to view the history that the Thames has witnessed as a gigantic tale of greatness. It is also why, on my reading, he is too engaged within the ideological frame which that tale of greatness implies to be deliberately playing out the contradictory double entendres contained, for example, in 'germs of Empire'. (Are germs seeds or disease?) But through his language, Conrad has given us as readers a chance to 'read against the grain' of the narrator's ring of confidence, to recognize ironies contained within the positive rhetoric. In sensing the way the language works *against* the ostensible affirmative message, we hit upon one of the core insights of Conrad's practice as a writer. Language, rarely 'pure', always subject to ideological contamination, nevertheless functions both to lie and tell the truth, cover up and reveal, at the same time. The passage points us towards one of the most forcefully addressed questions of the novel: the relationship between language, power, and belief.

Taking the framing narrator at his own word, though, history is a glorious tale. So *Heart of Darkness*, we may start to think, will be an appropriately adventurous and glorious history, easily available to 'us', present as 'abiding memory': 'Indeed nothing is easier for a [sailor] than to evoke the great spirit of the past'. Does 'evoke' mean recall, or even retell as a yarn? Doesn't this passage 'evoke' in us memories, however unspecific, of other stories, of which, we can expect, this will be a type? As readers living in a particular cultural and historical milieu, we are always evoking other texts to help us come to terms with the one we are presently reading, whether a fairy story, newspaper article, or nineteenth-century realist novel. This is what recent criticism has referred to as 'intertextuality'. No work is an island. Each must be read through the 'mesh' of our other reading, which doesn't prevent each also being unique, at the same time that it is a rereading of others. This field of reference need not be a specific earlier work, though it could be that too. (For example, we cannot not think of *Hamlet* if we read or see Stoppard's *Rosencrantz and Guildenstern Are Dead*.) Less directly allusive, though no less potent for our reading, are the interrelations with other works suggested when we read, for example, the opening of *Anna Karenina* or *Pride and Prejudice* and think of the literary type 'broken marriage' or 'wealthy man seeks beautiful wife'. However reductive these narrative schemes can be – 'the Oedipus situation', 'the journey of discovery', 'the great escape' – the reader hears their echo even in the most complex work, and draws inferences about the work from them. Thus every character and situation of a novel, however individualized, is endowed with properties which are not so much stated by the text as brought to it, read into it, by the reader, drawing on his or her knowledge not only of the practical world at large but of other texts. How much knowledge of what we call 'ordinary life' or 'the real world' comes to us in fact mediated through narrative texts!

What is the 'intertextual' relation proposed by the framing narrator's opening meditation? Surely nineteenth-century adventures, the tales of R. L. Stevenson, Rider Haggard, or Kipling, or tales from schoolboy magazines – stories of empire, stories of adventure. I would also suggest that Conrad's strategy in using the anonymous first-person narrator is in part to evoke this intertextual sense – in order subsequently to subvert it.

You may now be thinking I am making too much of a relatively short passage, delivered moreover by a narrator who turns out to be secondary. Two points are worth considering: the high importance of opening pages in our readerly negotiation with and expectations of the work; and also Conrad's own comments.

When *Heart of Darkness* first came out in 1899 in three-part serial publication in *Blackwood's Magazine*, Conrad's socialist aristocrat friend Robert Cunninghame Graham responded enthusiastically. Conrad replied with thanks and a warning:

> There are two more instalments in which the idea is so wrapped up in secondary notions that you – even you! may miss it. And also you must

remember that I don't start with an abstract notion. I start with
definite images and as their rendering is true some little effect is
produced. So far this note struck chimes in with your conviction. Mais
après? There is an après.[2]

Conrad's point is that meanings are suggested rather than stated,
that ideas emerge through details, are not easily abstractable. The
effect is the almost insidious absorption of meanings. In the case of
the framing narrator, we are implicitly invited to accept not just an
adventure story but, more importantly for Conrad's purposes, a
way of looking at history which embodies an ideological frame of
reference we would now call imperialist or colonialist.

No sooner do we have this rhetorical prelude than Marlow's
voice interrupts, breaking the silence with 'And this also . . . has been
one of the dark places of the earth'. Then the first narrator gives us
what in the light of the subsequent story is a striking account of
Marlow's storytelling habits. In effect it is a warning about our
reading practices. What are we told about Marlow which makes us
start to question our assumptions about the tale? And Marlow
himself: how do we 'read' him?

Look at the narrator's description of him (pp. 29–30). **In what
ways does Marlow not 'represent his class'? What is characteristic
about his stories, and how do they differ from ordinary sailors' tales?**

DISCUSSION

Marlow is identified through difference. Compared to others aboard
the *Nellie*, though not to the seafarers we have just heard about, he is
a wanderer, an adventurer. But unlike other seamen, he is one who
embraces rather than complacently ignores the unknown and uncertain. His tales are equally problematic:

> The yarns of seamen have a direct simplicity, the whole meaning of
> which lies within the shell of a cracked nut. But Marlow was not
> typical (if his propensity to spin yarns be excepted), and to him the
> meaning of an episode was not inside like a kernel but outside,
> enveloping the tale which brought it out only as a glow brings out a
> haze, in the likeness of one of those misty halos that sometimes are
> made visible by the spectral illumination of moonshine.   (p. 30)

The image, like its referent (its 'meaning'), is at once precise and
intangible. What is asserted is that Marlow's stories do not contain
their meanings positively, at the end of their telling, like an answer to
a riddle or a moral tag to a proverb, bur rather evoke them in the
course of the telling. Perhaps Marlow's tale will have no end and
its meaning remain 'hazy'. We are at least being warned against
expecting a conclusive summation.

And what do you make of his interruption itself? Read carefully
Marlow's version of the earlier imperial conquest (pp. 30–2). Why
do you think Conrad has Marlow talk suddenly about the Roman
conquest of Britain? How far does the imagery he uses of light and
dark, illumination and ignorance, for example, correspond to earlier
uses by the framing narrator? How does Marlow's sense of the past
and conquest compare to the latter's?

DISCUSSION

Generally, the introduction of the Roman conquest offers a radical
shift of perspective on Britain hitherto seen as a conquering proud
nation. It implies history is not monolithic. Your view of it depends
on where you are standing. Victories and conquests feel different for
the vanquished. Conrad wants to shock us into this recognition by
presenting conquest from the disturbing aspect of Britain as the dark
and ignorant conquered land. Marlow's abrupt interruption undercuts both the narrator's confident rhetoric and its historical supposi-
tions. While the narrator sees the past as a constantly present tale of
fortitude and glory, Marlow offers a stark alternative. Like Africa
now, Britain, too, has been (the tense almost suggests contempor-
aneity) a dark place. In his account of the Roman conquest of Britain,
Marlow adopts the oppositional imagery of the first narrator –
lightness and dark, illumination and ignorance, conquest and conquered, civilized and savage – only to invert its reference. Britain is
now the victim, not the perpetrator, of 'historic acts' – but in either
role is still the subject of tales for conquerors to 'brag about'.

Is Marlow merely saying that history repeats itself? Certainly, if
Britain is the referent for all the images of detestation and savagery,
this contradicts the narrator's implicit view of history as a glorious
progress. But more than this, in positing a different view of history,
Marlow's narration prepares us for a much more radical idea. In an
act of challenging inversion, Marlow suggests Britain *is still*, in a
sense, one of the dark places.

The sudden shift of perspective which Marlow opens up for us
also challenges any complacent view of 'historic acts' of conquest:

> It was just robbery with violence, aggravated murder on a grand scale
> and men going at it blind – as is very proper for those who tackle a
> darkness. The conquest of the earth, which mostly means the taking it
> away from those who have a different complexion or slightly flatter
> noses than ourselves, is not a pretty thing when you look into it too
> much.   (pp. 31–2)

Not only is there a reversal of referents – Britain becomes
the conquered of another's Empire – but also the *judgements*

attached to certain activities are also reversed. Colonialization, civilizing progress, and dreams of empire become mass murder, robbery with violence, and nightmare. Bearers of the torch flounder in blindness (a motif we ought to remember).

But then, after Marlow's outspoken attack on activities which his listeners might be made to feel complicit in ('flatter noses than *ourselves*' – my italics), something rather odd happens. He adds:

> What redeems it is the idea only. An idea at the back of it; not a sentimental idea – something you can set up, and bow down before, and offer a sacrifice to . . .   (p. 32)

What do you make of this qualification? Is Marlow modifying his attack, or contradicting it? Is he implying that there *is after all* some justification for this brutal 'conquest of the earth'? Or is 'redeem' different from 'justify'? And what sort of 'idea' is it? It is too early in the book to get firm answers to these questions – if it offers any – but we'd do well to let the questions echo in our minds as we read on. Doesn't the phrase, 'something to bow down before', in fact, sound vaguely familiar? You'll recall that the word 'idol' was used in the framing narrator's description of Marlow's pose. I can't do much at the moment with this verbal echo, but – and I think this is how Conrad's creating of 'little effects' works – the text throws up verbal parallels, echoes, contrasts, which suggest links but do not name the relations; they signify without clear referents. Whether and how these get 'named' or articulated we will have to wait to see.

Soon afterwards we're given another warning from the framing narrator about Marlow's competence as a story-teller which may bear upon this referential uncertainty: 'We were fated to hear about one of Marlow's inconclusive experiences'. And yet immediately this is qualified by a remark from Marlow about the sort of tale he is launching into. For him, his journey up-river into the interior was 'to the farthest point of navigation and the culminating point of my experience'. Taken by the reader as a comment on the narrative itself, it sounds as if the end of the journey will in both senses be the end (final point and purpose) of the tale itself, and that we will be delivered of the wisdom gained by 'The Man Who Came Back'.

So after the first narrator's exposition, Marlow's intervention has set up a force of narrative 'disturbance' which generates the need for his story to 'resolve' in some way. Another feature of Marlow's intervention which I find troubling is its motivation: '"And this also," said Marlow suddenly . . .'. Why 'and'? **Do you think Marlow is in mid-conversation, offering a rejoinder to the narrator's previous remarks? If so, how do you make sense of the narrator saying he is** 'meditating in silence'? How do you explain the sort of continuity the text implies?

DISCUSSION

I find this a problem. It is as if his remark is a rejoinder — which is indeed, I think, how we read it. But like the others on board, the narrator has been meditating, not speaking aloud — and nor does his literary rhetoric suggest to me the spoken. So this continuity of 'dialogue' — which significantly contradicts the narrator's impression of illustrious history — is a continuity only on the written page for the reader. Perhaps this suggests that so shared is their sense of community and common assumption that they intuitively know what the others would say and are in silent dialogue. But Marlow later refers to the narrator's thoughts as speech ('You say knights'). How is this? Is there any significance we can attach to these continuities and the confusing status of the text as variously written, spoken, or thought which they imply? Unless Conrad has just slipped up, the problem remains one we will have to ponder.

(iii) Conrad and Binary Thinking

The constellation of images emerging in these opening pages — light/dark, past/present, civilized/savage, for example — raise a further, quite far-ranging issue. So far we've been talking in terms of binary oppositions. Perhaps this structural way of thinking is inherent not only in the terms offered by this work but, much more deeply ingrained than this, informs in a thoroughly assimilated way, a mode of thinking central to modern Western culture. Oppositional, binary thinking is so much a part of our everyday lives — man/woman, good/bad, old/young — that we no longer recognize it as an imposed structure of thought. We tend to 'naturalize' it. We claim (or rather less consciously than 'claim', assume) as normal, natural, 'the way things are', what are in fact intellectual, *ideational* constructions which we, fully acculturated, impose on the material world as if they had actual material substance. Of course, as an everyday mode of perceiving and organizing ourselves and the space, people, and objects around us, this opposition carries with it the conviction of the substantial. Things are in or out, standing or sitting, left or right, children or adults. But these ways of organizing the world conceptually sometimes trap us into assuming that what are essentially metaphorical categories actually describe the real world of things which exist in relation to one another as an infinitely graduated series of differences, of things constantly in play of variance.

Perhaps we mistake metaphorical ways of thinking for 'the real thing'. In George Eliot's *Middlemarch*, we are warned against our facility for articulating the world in terms of metaphors and then believing in their substantiality. 'For all of us, grave or light, get our thoughts entangled in metaphors and act fatally on the strength of them.'[3] Applied to *Heart of Darkness*, I think we will come to see that Conrad finds in these binary images a powerful tool which, when re-evaluated, can provide the means for a radical and disturbing critique of our too-easily assumed cultural norms. Is the civilized really savage? Are ideals really graven idols? Is faithfulness a sham? Is darkness, the unknown, to be found in the other or in ourselves?

Ultimately we might want to go beyond the critique which Conrad offers by means of these terms in order to question their assumptions as terms. We might, that is, want to question their substantiality which, for all his re-evaluation of them, Conrad endorses by adopting them. Put simply, do the categories of, say, civilized and savage in Conrad's work remain intact as ideas, surviving his critique of their specific application? To try to answer this would be to place Conrad into the history of his time and the necessary limits to thought which his history offered him. Conrad offers through Marlow a critique of one set of ideological assumptions, and seeing how he achieves this will be a major concern for us. But we ought to push further too and try to criticize the critique, 'deconstruct' it by subjecting its terms to our own questions.

With Marlow on the edge of his narration, let me briefly summarize. Our focus has been shifted from one narrator to another. With this, our expectations and norms constructed by the text, or inferred by us through our intertextual awareness, have been altered. Marlow, both in the kind of story he tells and what we can deduce about his point of view about his subject, disturbs the tentative 'known' balance we have established with the first-person narrator. At the same time, a series of associated images has been foregrounded, which through repetition by both narrators implies an increasing richness of significance, even if at the moment we cannot confidently nail all of it down. Lightness/darkness is the most obvious pair, but illumination/blindness, idea/idol, civilized/savage, conqueror/conquest, vital/dead, and dream/nightmare are others.

However we may come to judge these sets of images and their application to specific referents, they articulate a network of thematic concerns. Their frequency of occurrence, their symbolic resonance suggest this already, and they will reverberate throughout the rest of the novel: themes of exploration and self-exploration; the nature of civilized life; the need for and the function of ideological (or if you will excuse the misspelling) idealogical 'justification' for actions; the ends or the end of stories.

The next chapter will attend closely to the episodes leading up to Marlow's departure for Africa (pp. 32–9). After a brief reference to his boyhood fascination for maps, Marlow recounts a series of incidents including his turning to his aunt for aid; his trip to the European capital which we infer to be Brussels; his visit to Company headquarters; and a seemingly digressive insertion into the narrative, the story of Fresleven, the Company captain Marlow replaces. Recalling Conrad's statement about 'secondary notions', I suggest we hesitate before dismissing these pages as being of marginal narrative interest. They are important for what they tell us obliquely of Marlow's self-presentation – and of course what we think of *that* will determine how we view his subsequent narrative. Furthermore, they are interesting because of the way the 'slight' episodes introduce very important themes.

Having taken careful note of your reading of pages 32–9, you should go on to complete your first reading of the novel. Although the shape of this Guide will broadly follow Marlow's journey in its consideration of specific incidents, a complete first reading will be assumed before you embark upon Chapter 4 of the Guide.

3. Senses of Place

(i) Mapping the Scene

Maps are more than transcriptions of physical space. For Marlow, as for the young Conrad,[1] they are the spur to dreams of adventure and exploration. And the blanker the maps, the greater the imaginative space they offer him. They prompt his search for employment with the European trading company, and their persistent power to fascinate is twice reiterated in Marlow's account of the period up to his embarkation for Africa. **Think about the two descriptions of maps** (pp. 33, 36) and consider what they tell us of his image of Africa. How geographically or historically specific do you think Marlow's description of Africa is? In his talk about maps, what attitude does he reveal towards the continent?

DISCUSSION

His perception is governed much more by the fascination for the unknown than for full cartographic precision. His idea of Africa is much more committed to (and fearful of) a space which his imagination can people than an already full and peopled place. On close scrutiny I do not find any concrete evidence of specific place or time. I am assuming that on a 'factual' level the maps depict the continent and particularly the course of the River Congo. The 'blank space' had been increasingly filled by colours, an allusion to the territorial claims of European colonialist powers which took place in the 'Scramble for Africa' in the early 1880s. The French (blue), the Portuguese and Italians (orange and green), the Germans (purple), and the Belgians (yellow) can be identified alongside the 'vast amount of red' of the British, 'good to see at any time because one knows that some real work is done in there'. We will have cause to return to the implications of this last phrase: even without naming it, Marlow seems to be setting Britain apart from the other colonial powers.

I say 'Africa' and the 'Congo'. But we will soon discover that nowhere in the whole novel are they explicitly named. Nor are subsequent locations, the Company Station, the Central Station, Kurtz's Inner Station, given their corresponding geographical names – Matadi, Kinchassa, Stanley Falls. A related problem is the temporal displacement, the historical anonymity, you might say, of Marlow's tale. We can try to postulate a temporal setting for his trip – and we can draw for our evidence on subsequent references to the Company, modelled on the Société Anonyme Belge pour le Commerce du Haut-Congo (formed in 1888), and the Eldorado Exploring Company (modelled on a Katanga expedition of 1890). Even the Martini-Henry and Winchester rifles, in such cavalier use, suggest the 1870s or 1880s. We deduce that Marlow's trip is roughly contemporaneous with Conrad's Congo journey in 1890. The valuable work of the critic Norman Sherry has established the personal, historical, and geographical correspondences between *Heart of Darkness* and Conrad's Africa.[2] By the late 1880s Africa, specifically the Congo area, was much more fully colonized, settlements were more numerous and extended – the maps, in other words, were more intricately elaborated – than any impression we get from Marlow's account.

When fictionalizing, Conrad avoided 'realistic' (historical, geographical) specificity, and transposed Marlow's Africa back into an anachronistic and hence more anonymous space. **Why do you think Conrad insists on this sort of 'blankness'? Is the later description of the 'sepulchral city' any different? What are the effects of this anonymity?**

DISCUSSION

I have noted some possible narrative functions:

1 Non-specificity can work to extend the range and relevance of Marlow's experience, universalizing the impact of Conrad's critique.
2 It can highlight broad, even elemental qualities of experience, unconstrained by the limiting particularities of realistic detail.
3 'Blankness' can reinforce the sense of mystery, the unknown darkness to be explored in the narrative.
4 It can engage me as a reader much more, as I imaginatively fill in the 'blank spaces' of the narrative.

On the last point, indeed, we have Conrad's own validation. In a letter to his friend Richard Curle, he writes about the drawbacks of explicitness:

> Didn't it ever occur to you, my dear Curle, that I knew what I was doing in leaving the facts of my life and even of my tales in the background? Explicitness, my dear fellow, is fatal to the glamour of all artistic work, robbing it of all suggestiveness, destroying all illusion.[3]

But wait a minute! 'Glamour'? It recalls the 'glamour' Marlow projects into the blank spaces on the maps of his youth. Do we as readers of books re-enact with an equivalent fascination the sort of filling out of blankness that Marlow is charmed into? Remember how emphatically Marlow's description of the snaking river seems to insist on an almost Edenic temptation. Both spaces, the fictive narrative and the place, are objects which invite the complicit imagination.

Perhaps 'Africa', represented on a map as a blankness slowly being filled up, is not so much a physical, geographical space, as an imaginative one, available to whatever dreams (or fears) may be inscribed upon it by an engaged Western observer. In addition to those functions suggested above, then, non-specificity or anonymity would be a sign of a kind of emptiness, an 'absence' construed as exotic 'otherness', the dark 'unknown', fascinating for the possibilities of imaginative exploitation and appropriation it offers. I use 'exploitation' deliberately to draw an analogy between the acts of imagination and those of political and economic colonization. In *Heart of Darkness* maps might be thought to stand at the intersection of these two spheres, as the material emblem of both activities.

Maps do transcribe physical space. They also in a sense *inscribe* it, with names, boundary lines, and even (if we think of cartographic projections) a perspective from which to view it. Maps and map-making are the result and also a tool of territorial possession. As explorers discover new land, they map it both to claim it and to move in it and control it better.

But what does 'discover' mean here? When I say 'Livingstone discovered the Victoria Falls in 1855', what am I saying? Or rather, what am I assuming in saying it? That the area was not peopled, that the river did not exist, before his arrival? Well, no. But it was not known; at least it was not known to us Europeans. Livingstone saw it 'for the first time' and gave it a name (for reasons honorific rather than for physical resemblance). Everybody knows about it now, and by that name. In other words, in claiming to 'discover' what must therefore by definition be a hitherto 'unknown' land or people, and by mapping and naming it as testimony, am I not concealing the fact of expropriation? At least, in using the word 'discover' and giving names and borders to 'blank' spaces, I make it a good deal easier to impose my will (and language) because 'there was nothing there before I came'.

Thinking of 'Africa' as represented by a blankness slowly filling up, an 'absence', an unknown dark interior, enables Conrad, Marlow, and us to construe it, to appropriate it imaginatively or actually. We can then give it whatever attributes we want to – as the mysterious, the primal, the 'mute wilderness', the site of 'forgotten and brutal instincts' and unspeakable rites. And might there be a structural analogy between this kind of spatial 'absence' and the 'otherness' of its black inhabitants who are similarly and powerfully construed by Marlow, who are spoken for, but almost never speak? They too are 'absences'. By 'absence', I am thinking of how, often, works can reveal as much implicitly as they do explicitly, when we look at traces in them as a cat owner might a feather on the carpet. We should ask of works: what is not said, what cannot be said, who or what remains unspoken in the work, 'significantly absent' from it? And how is this absence constructed? It is not a perfect analogue, but imagine a dinner table conversation where it was known that one of the party has been recently bereaved. Death may never be mentioned, the feelings of the bereaved never alluded to, but both would affect the tone and behaviour of the other guests; both would be structuring absences in the conversation. **And are there other significant 'absences' in the novel? Think about the women.**

I have offered one view of the function of maps and their fascination. Here is a different reading from an article by Frederick Crews that has its starting point in this same fascination.

> Just consider: a sunken, ascetic narrator who fervently believes that women should be kept quarantined 'in that beautiful world of their own, lest ours gets worse', tells us that he felt irrationally compelled to visit a dark and mysterious continent. . . . Since childhood he had yearned to visit this area, and now at great risk . . . he arrived via a river described as 'an immense snake uncoiled, with . . . its tail lost in the depths of the land.' . . . he eventually found the much-respected Kurtz in a state of depravity, accompanied by a savage mistress in a wilderness. . . . Now withered and helpless, and rescued by the narrator from 'certain midnight dances ending with unspeakable rites', Kurtz acknowledged 'the horror' of his experience and died . . .
>
> If such a plot were recounted to a psychoanalyst as a dream . . . the interpretation would be beyond doubt. The exposed sinner at the heart of darkness would be an image of the father, accused of sexual 'rites' with the mother. The dreamer is preoccupied with the primal scene, which he symbolically interrupts. The journey into the maternal body is both voyeuristic and incestuous, and the rescue of the father is more defiant and supplantive than tender and restitutive. The closing episode with the 'phantom' woman in a sarcophagal setting would be the dreamer-son's squaring of accounts with his dead mother. . . . Only one complaint against the sainted mother is allowed to reach expression: the son tells her with devious truthfulness that the dying sinner's last word ('horror!') was 'your name'.[4]

This raises a general question which can't yet be answered, perhaps, but which you should be thinking about. It is an interpretation of an allegorical sort, seeing Marlow's journey as a journey into the sexual traumas of the unconscious. Does this new psychological dimension of the meaning of 'darkness' help you to make sense of the quality of fascination which Marlow shows? Crews is not alone in seeing the novel as a journey into the psychic interior. Albert Guerard, for example, has argued that:

> substantially and in its central emphasis *Heart of Darkness* concerns Marlow (projection to whatever great or small degree of a more irrecoverable Conrad) and his journey towards and through certain facets or potentialities of self . . . [It is] the night-journey into the unconscious and confrontation of an entity [Kurtz] within the self.[5]

You might think about the virtues and difficulties of this sort of psychological reading.

In the next few pages, Marlow recounts the preparations for the Congo, which I've already described as incidentals – but incidentals

well worth our consideration. **What impression do you get of
Marlow in his description of himself gaining his appointment? What
self-presentation is implied by his 'loafing around' then calling on his
aunt for help?**

DISCUSSION

My first impression is of a masculine (macho?), knowing worldli-
ness, slightly embarrassed by recourse to a 'mere woman'. What
strikes me immediately is that Marlow establishes an ironic and
indeed self-ironic perspective on his experience. We have already
been informed by the framing narrator that Marlow is not like
'ordinary seamen'. Now Conrad contributes further to his characterization by having him reveal himself as self-mocking ('loafing
around'), worldly-wise ('I always went my own road'), and not
over-easily impressed ('I got my appointment – of course'). In other
words, what we can infer is that if his journey will be to 'the
culminating point' of his experience, it is not the journey (however
psychological or mythical) of a gullible innocent. If extremities of
experience are to be portrayed, we can at least trust Marlow's coolly
ironic voice not to exaggerate them. Although in the light of our
discussion in Chapter 2 we may not want to over-invest our confidence in the correctness of a narrator's judgements, nevertheless my
impression is of a man who presents himself as someone of physical
and moral restraint. This self-portrayal will heighten the impact on
us of those moments later in the narrative when his self-control
falters.

(ii) The Relevance of Fresleven

**The Fresleven digression is illustrative here. First, is it so 'digressive'?
How does it elaborate the relations of white men to black natives?
What does the story reveal about their attitudes towards one
another? Furthermore, what are you told about Marlow's response
to violent death? Finally, does the story in any way prefigure
Marlow's meeting with Kurtz?**

DISCUSSION

Taking the last question first, it does offer another narrative about a
white man confronting 'darkest Africa' and reacting extremely to it.
Moreover, it draws upon ideas which caricature a superstitious,
semi-deifying attitude of black natives to white men ('the supernatural being') and about murderous violence erupting in whites,

even in 'the gentlest, quietest creature'. It proposes that exposure to this alien environment threatens to release ordinary European whites from their 'natural' restraint.

The sense of the meaninglessness of the events surrounding Fresleven's death is matched, indeed mimicked, in the off-hand manner of Marlow's recounting of it. The very inappropriateness of tone seems aesthetically fitting. The absurd discrepancy of cause (a quarrel over two black hens) and effect (death and mad terror) is inversely rendered in its enormity by Marlow's ironic understatement. His almost callous detachment ('of course') deliberately underplays the horror and his tone asserts at once his self-presentation as 'worldly' and the arbitrariness of the act.

In both substance and language the Fresleven episode gives early warning to us of the quality of absurdity – the felt discrepancies of avowed aim to achievement, cause to effect – which so profoundly colours Marlow's experience of colonialism and his rendering of it. What happens on the thematic level (dislocation of significance, futility) is reflected linguistically in the disjunction between signified and signifier, the words used and what's actually referred to.

Like Fresleven's fate, but discrepant in the opposite direction, is the description of the fate of the hens (a minor issue, surely, except to the hens). The incident is trivial, the language imperial: 'the cause of progress got them, anyhow'. And in a rhetorical strategy which pervades the whole work, other potentially jingoistic phrases – 'the noble cause', 'the glorious affair', and even 'self-respect' – are exploited dialectically by Conrad. They both expose and deflate the actions to which they refer, and (back-firing, so to speak) through their inappropriateness undercut their own signifying force as language. Put briefly, not only is Fresleven's death not a 'glorious affair', but the very phrase, 'glorious affair', has by the same stroke been contaminated.

Generally, then, we can see how through the ironies of verbal disproportion Marlow's account underlines the senselessness of events. It thus disturbs our habitual assumption that the world is intelligible and ordered. Simultaneously, the vehicle for that subversion – language – itself does not escape intact from the ironies it has produced.

The Fresleven story is proleptic in two respects. It anticipates, as I said, elements in the Kurtz story. But also as an event in narrated time it occurs, strictly speaking, at a point some time subsequent to Marlow's visit to Company Headquarters. **Why does Conrad introduce the Fresleven story here, out of its 'real' place in the order of narrated time? Is it possible that Mr William Blackwood, Conrad's** magazine editor, thought the serial version could do with a little spicing up, a macabre joke, perhaps? Did Conrad have a less than perfect grasp of temporal order? Or – was Conrad interested in the juxtaposition between Marlow's visit to Company Headquarters and the finding of Fresleven's corpse?

DISCUSSION

It is possible that Mr Blackwood demanded dark relief in the story – but we don't have any written evidence for it, or for Blackwood's sense of humour. And it is possible that Conrad got his chronology confused. After all, Marlow says that 'months and months' afterwards he found Fresleven's corpse, but his subsequent narrative offers very little opportunity for Marlow to have done so – unless, glutton for punishment, he returned to Africa after his trip back to Europe. But the problem still remains – why interpose the Fresleven story here? It is surely more than likely that Conrad was interested in the juxtaposition of the two incidents. Do you see any parallels and continuities between Marlow's visit to the Company Headquarters and the pages preceding it? Note, for instance, the sense of the ominous, and the morbid taken for granted; a tone of ironic detachment – but this time with Marlow as its object; and finally, suggestions of a mythic dimension to the story.

Look at the following passage:

> In a very few hours I arrived in a city that always makes me think of a whited sepulchre. Prejudice no doubt. I had no difficulty in finding the Company's offices. It was the biggest thing in the town, and everybody I met was full of it. They were going to run an over-sea empire, and make no end of coin by trade.
>
> A narrow and deserted street in deep shadow, high houses, innumerable windows with venetian blinds, a dead silence, grass sprouting between the stones, imposing carriage archways right and left, immense double doors standing ponderously ajar. I slipped through one of these cracks, went up a swept and ungarnished staircase, as arid as a desert, and opened the first door I came to. Two women, one fat and the other slim, sat on straw-bottomed chairs, knitting black wool. (p. 35)

This passage comes within a paragraph of Marlow's description of Fresleven's corpse, 'the grass growing through his ribs was tall enough to hide his bones' – to which Conrad, unable to resist a further macabre twist of the knife, adds, 'They were all there'. Surely we're meant to hear the echo, visualize the parallelism, in 'dead silence, grass sprouting between the stones'. And in 'whited sepulchre' don't we pick up a fragment of Fresleven's parched bones? This 'flash-forward' to Fresleven (like the earlier flash-back from the modern day Thames to Roman Britain) insists on the juxtaposition of two narrative spaces (Africa, Europe) which can provoke unexpected and significant points of comparison otherwise obscured. Without the juxtaposition, the geographical and temporal separation of the scene in Africa and Europe might have reinforced earlier or generated new binary oppositions. We could then remain complacent in our cultural assumptions: Africa associated with darkness, death, madness, the exotic, the absurd; Europe associated with light, life, sanity, the familiar, the intelligible. But this is precisely what, in Chapter 2, we have found Conrad questioning. The narrative structure proposes, without stating explicitly, that such a division is deeply questionable. Moreover, the continuities between Africa and Europe emphasize the very presence of mortality in the heart of this thriving business capital, this 'whited sepulchre'. What does this last phrase convey to you? Doesn't it, with its biblical ring (from Matthew 23:27), conjoin this mortality with the ideas of lies and hypocrisy, suggesting something unwholesome about cosmopolitan Europe?

My view is that it does. Furthermore, this sense of the ominous is confirmed in the presence of 'the uncanny and fateful' two women knitting black wool. Even to Marlow they resemble the Virgilian Sybil 'guarding the door of Darkness'. Their similarity to two of the Classical mythological figures of Fate, Lachesis and Clotho, spinners of the thread of human lives, has often been remarked. They are knowing and indifferent, as sinister as the knitters sitting before the guillotine. This brings up another of those very general issues of interpretation of the novel – the place of myth in Conrad's conception of Africa.

(iii) Myth

Such literary allusions, Marlow's own comments ('I felt as though, instead of going to the centre of a continent, I was about to set off for the centre of the earth' (p. 39)), and references to 'pilgrims' and 'shades' have encouraged an important body of Conradian criticism which reads the whole work within a mythical framework of a classical journey to the Underworld.[6] Here is one such reading.

> Immediately preceding the real descent, Conrad devotes several paragraphs to explanation [. . .] of his special Hades. He carefully separates Africa from modern civilization by describing machinery rusting uselessly on a hillside. . . . As Marlow travels up the river on the steam launch the natives are literally downtrodden blacks, but they resemble those [in Dante's City of Dis] who are violent against their neighbors. . . . The Russian trader that Marlow and his company encounter appears to be a heretic. Conrad actually calls him a 'harlequin',

a verbal resemblance that is perhaps more than coincidental. . . .
Conrad's Hell is mythical. . . . Perhaps [Kurtz] is not symbolically
fixed in ice [the fate of Dante's Alberti brothers, guilty of treason]
because Conrad wished to suggest that evil as he was, a still worse fate
awaited him . . .

It is a journey through the underworld for purposes of instruction as
well as entertainment. . . . The strength of the story lies not in the
suspense it develops but in the power of its clear moral insight . . .[7]

This view offers a general – and perhaps generalizing – reading of
Marlow's journey. Even if you don't yet want to tackle it in detail,
what do you think of this kind of reading, which sees in *Heart of
Darkness* an allegory of a moral or spiritual journey, alluding to
Dante's? (For my own response to this, you might look at the
accompanying footnote 8.)

Allusions are one thing, systematic mythologies and allegories
another. Allusions can at once propose and frustrate readings;
allegories tend to embody definitive ones. It is true that Marlow may
portray himself at times (particularly in the first third of the book) in
mythical or romanticized terms, rescuing Kurtz whom he compares
to an 'enchanted princess sleeping in a fabulous castle' (p. 77); or
heroizing himself as victim, as Roman gladiator, hailing farewell to
the two knitters with 'Morituri te salutant' ('Those who are about to
die salute you!'). This mythologizing is not that unusual – don't we
all sometimes, in our daily lives, cast ourselves in roles, saying or
thinking, 'We can be heroes. Just for one day'? Certainly in Marlow's
case, that does not preclude self-irony. Nor does it make Conrad's
account of Marlow's actual experiences (any more than it would the
actual course of our lives) conform strictly to the romantic or mythic
models he (or we) have fleetingly invoked. The interpenetration of
the everyday and the mythic is suggested, but the one doesn't replace
the other.

(iv) The Company

The 'uncanny' modulates into the morbid as Marlow visits the old
Company doctor (pp. 37–8). **How does Marlow react to his treatment by the doctor? What does it suggest to you about his sense of
allegiance to the Company?**

DISCUSSION

Interestingly, the cold detachment of Marlow's account of Fresleven
– which we may feel has something of the self-dramatizing 'stiff
upper lip' about it – is replicated in the scientific 'disinterestedness' of
this phrenologist and alienist. That last term is a technical one (used

from the 1860s on) for a psychologist, but it is also fortuitously one that underlines this distanced perspective. Marlow, his own sanity under scrutiny, becomes a specimen of scientific curiosity, an object of knowledge. As such, he is the unwilling participant in the doctor's experiments in pursuit of the 'neutral' and 'rational' 'interests of science'. It is a 'simple formality', a brief visit. But it is not one that today's readers of Conrad are able to pass over with any ease. Reading the incident in our own time (that is, after 1945), can we help but register its prophetic anticipation of other, twentieth-century, testimonies to barbarities done in the name of science? Just as those 'scientific experiments' were inseparable from the ideology and practices of Nazism, for example, so the Doctor's 'objective' scientific interest is, by his own admission, explicitly tied to the other profits of colonization.

In brief, the incident reveals (though Marlow could hardly say so) that no sooner does he enter the employment of the Company, than he becomes complicit in its processes and structures, but less as a controlling subject than an *object* of them. Marlow, the detached observer, is now also observed; aware, in his irritated manner, of his own potential reification, his 'alienation'.

Incidentally, for Conrad this scientific interest was uncomfortably close to home. A letter in 1881 from his uncle and guardian, Tadeusz Bobrowski, makes the following considerate request on behalf of a friend, a Mr Kopernicki:

> He is engaged on a great work which has already brought him European fame: 'Comparative studies of human races based on types of skulls'. This particular branch of science is called 'Craniology'. He earnestly requests you to collect during your voyages skulls of natives, writing on each one whose skull it is and the place of origin. When you have collected a dozen or so skulls write to me and I will obtain from him information as to the best way of dispatching them to Cracow.[9]

There is no surviving record of Conrad's reply.

(v) Charlie's Aunt

Marlow's disconcerting interview with the doctor is followed by his visit to take leave of his aunt. It is an episode, slight in itself, which in my view signals a hardly-mentioned yet central factor in the narrative economy of the novel. It is another 'signifying absence' – the (almost erased) place and representation of women in Marlow's story. We will discuss this more fully in Chapter 6. Now, though, I'd like you to consider some preliminary questions. **Having reread the episode (pp. 38–9), would you agree with me that Marlow finds the meeting somehow awkward? Try to locate sources for what he calls** his discomfort. And what is the effect of Conrad juxtaposing this scene with the previous interview with the doctor?

DISCUSSION

Two grounds for his discomfort occur to me. Marlow's male sense of himself causes embarrassment at the idea that a woman's string-pulling can get him a job. Furthermore, he is scornful about what he sees as her complacent chatter about his forthcoming work.

The previous scene revealed how a disinterested ('male') scientific knowledge ('discoveries') is both a product of but also a justification for the processes of colonization. Marlow's aunt's view, matching it in some ways, reveals a 'female' version of this, showing a naïve idealizing of the same processes. With the enthusiasm of an arm-chair missionary, she sees in them a civilizing and Christianizing purpose which elevates a 'worker' like Marlow to an 'emissary of light [. . .] a lower sort of apostle'. Juxtaposing positivistic science and religion, the text *reveals* what Marlow does not and cannot tell us: the two are not mutually incompatible, antagonistic interests. Rather, both fields of discourse offer ideological justification for what Marlow identifies, already at this stage in his experience of it, as the crude workings of the profit motive. Ironically, he differentiates and disassociates himself from colonialism's ideological manifestations at the very moment he is engaging with it himself. Specimen within the one discourse, rather patronizing critic of the other, he is uncomfortably implicated in both.

This discomfort provokes Marlow into one of his relatively infrequent moralizing pronouncements uttered in the generalizing present tense, which it is worth looking at here:

> It's queer how out of touch with truth women are. They live in a world of their own, and there had never been anything like it, and never can be. It is too beautiful altogether, and if they were to set it up it would go to pieces before the first sunset. Some confounded fact we men have been living contentedly with ever since the day of creation would start up and knock the whole thing over.   (p. 39)

How would you describe Marlow's tone? Who does he mean by 'we men' – those in the Company, those on the *Nellie*? Try reading between his lines. Might Marlow's attitude to his aunt tell us more about *his* position?

DISCUSSION

I find his tone rather patronizing: Marlow and 'we men' knowing what the truth is, and knowing too that women are too beautifully naïve to recognize it. But the implied male solidarity of 'we men' seems puzzling. His experiences with the male Company, so to speak, have made him distinctly uncomfortable. When his aunt says naïve jingoistic things which implicate him in compromising ways, do you think it's possible that he's uncomfortable because he does not like what he's hearing about himself? Could his irritation be trying to hit a moving target? If so, his aunt (and 'naïve women') become the object of a displaced anger at the contradictions he feels in his *own* position *vis à vis* the Company. By sleight of hand, as it were, the women are made the useful object for his mild scorn, which has as much to do with *his* situation as with the nature of women. But he can't say that, or even think it. Instead, he resorts to a cultural cliché.

I would like you to consider Marlow's representation of women in this more complicated light and bear it in mind for when we come to consider later his interview with Kurtz's Intended.

At the moment, to sum up this chapter, let us recall the following points:

1 Marlow's fascination for maps introduced us to several issues in the novel – possible reasons for the novel's geographical anonymity; maps as blank spaces to be filled by our imaginations; and the possibilities of a psychological and mythical reading of Marlow's journey.
2 the Fresleven story, which foregrounds the idea of mortality and the sense of absurdity at times attendant upon it.
3 the interviews with the Company and aunt which reveal Marlow's discomfort at sensing the contradictions and complicity in his position, and the role he then finds for women to displace and accommodate this discomfort.

And on the stylistic level:

4 the strategy of juxtaposition which problematizes if it doesn't completely erode clear and comfortable binary oppositions.
5 Marlow's prevailing tone of knowing, ironic detachment, which tends to suggest rather than state these things. For the reader, like Marlow, they're more sensed than argued out.

Before concluding, and to introduce the main concern of my next chapter, Conrad's portrayal of colonialism, I'd like to pause on one of these points, the pervasive if absurd sense of mortality. Do we just want to rest with this idea? It is not, for example, a particularly shattering revelation to be told that, whoever and wherever we are, 'in the midst of life we are in death'. Nor that life throws up absurd and seemingly unintelligible occurrences. Indeed, there's a danger that our very acknowledgement of these things will empty them of their potency. 'The meaninglessness of the Universe? How true! . . . More coffee?' While we can find in Conrad's writing (particularly in his letters)[10] corroboration for the view that his was an altogether metaphysical, all-embracing nihilism, to locate the sense of mortality and absurdity at this level is to ignore the very concrete roots and identifications of it in Marlow's (and Conrad's) experiential knowledge of Africa and its colonization. We have begun to see how Marlow renders this 'absurdity' — through narrative strategies and ironic discourse marked by deflection, displacement, and deferred meaning. Do not these stylistic traits correlate precisely to the *mediated* nature of imperialist colonial practice?

These stylistic traits of indirection will raise an important political question. Is there a correlation between them and the subject-matter they render, the mediated, indirect nature of imperialist colonizing practice? By its very nature, imperialism often works at arm's length. Like its agent the doctor, or as we shall see, the French man-of-war 'firing into a continent', distance and indirection are primary means by which imperialism conceals from itself the true nature of its own activity, whether it is reflected in Kurtz's egomania or the brutalities of physical exploitation. So not surprisingly, direct connections aren't always visible.

But for all the process of self-delusion or sublimation, connections do exist between Europe and Africa, the 'civilized' and the 'savage'. Marlow's experience in Africa has revealed this to him. In a surreal, imagistic flash, connections are (however obscurely) made by him, even if it takes his narrating of the experience for the connections to be potentially understood. As he chases after Kurtz, he recalls,

> I had some imbecile thoughts. The knitting old woman with the cat obtruded herself upon my memory as a most improper person to be sitting at the other end of such an affair.   (p. 106)

In the sepulchral city death is present, but only in signs and symbols like the old women knitting. This might propose to us that the city is not the site of actual death but the source of it, the agent for its actuality elsewhere. The real meaning of Brussels lies in Africa. This Marlow senses, without being able to articulate the links. But the connection is there.

Are there other ways in which the text might tell us more about these connections than Marlow can? It is with this question that the next chapter is concerned. It will concentrate on a discussion of key episodes from pages 39–92, which you should now reread.

4. Colonialism; Semi-colonialism

Each gunshot opens another outlet for French industry. More than one worker who weaves cloth in some obscure factory only has work, perhaps, because a victory has pacified a whole country and allowed thousands to become part of our markets.[1]

(i) Leopold's Congo

Steal a little and they throw you in jail,
Steal a lot and they make you king.[2]

Explosions and economics are a central configuration of the civilizing mission in Africa which *Heart of Darkness* records. A mythic reading of the novel (such as Evans' Dantean sort discussed above, Ch. 3, pp. 31–2) cannot, in my view, encompass this configuration: it 'mythologizes' historical realities. The mythic interpretation has to evoke a cosmology of finely-tuned moral discriminations to account for the fact that Kurtz is *not* found by Marlow frozen in a lake of ice for his sins. At the very least this betrays an uncertain grasp of climatology. Further, it dissolves into abstraction Conrad's experience of the specific form of colonial imperialism Leopold II practised in his Congo Free State for two decades from 1885. I am not using the term 'imperialism' as a mere swear-word. Rather, I mean the specific territorial conquests made by the industrialized European nations in their 'Scramble for Africa' in the second half of the nineteenth century. The historical causes and nature of this imperial expansion have been the subject of much critical debate.[3] Suffice it to say that what was unusual about Leopold II's imperial presence in the Congo was that it became his personal territorial possession (rather than the Belgian State's). It was, in fact, recognized as such by the Berlin Conference of 1885, which arbitrated over European territorial ambitions in Africa, dividing the spoils primarily with the aim of averting conflict among the competing European nations. Moreover, Leopold pursued his Congo interests in the name of philanthropy and anti-slavery. As he himself stated:

The mission which the agents of the State have to accomplish on the

Congo is a noble one. They have to continue the development of civilization in the centre of Equatorial Africa, receiving their inspiration directly from Berlin and Brussels. Placed face to face with primitive barbarism, grappling with sanguinary customs that date back thousands of years, they are obliged to reduce these gradually. They must accustom the population to general laws, of which the most needful and the most salutary is assuredly that of work.[4]

The ironies of such rhetoric were not lost on Conrad.

The Berlin Conference circumscribed Leopold's absolute personal rule over almost one million square miles of Africa by regulations which guaranteed free trade among European nations and companies there (and the forbidding of differential dues). By 1890, however, with the sanction of the Brussels Conference, he took the power to establish trade tariffs (effectively controlling trade through setting up concession companies controlled by his personal representatives). To exploit fully the wealth of the Congo State, he instituted a 'labour tax' on natives in the form of forty hours per month of forced labour. In practice this was brutally and arbitrarily exacted by the chiefs of the concession companies with the ruthless encouragement of Leopold's local army. Increased production of ivory and rubber was their only priority, physical mutilation and abuse their method.

The exacting of a tax on Africans was not unique to Leopold. In most colonies the colonialist government levied a 'hut tax', payable in cash, which had the effect of compelling Africans to abandon their indigenous economic practices of subsistence farming or hunting to become wage labourers. This establishing of a labour force and a very rudimentary money economy might have encouraged the development of a native market for European manufactured goods. However, Leopold had little interest in establishing native Africans as potential consumers, since he had very little to sell them. Indeed one of the early reports exposing the crude economic 'robbery with violence' was E. D. Morel's revelations in 1904 demonstrating that Congo exports far exceeded imports.[5] In return for a vast outflow of profits to Leopold, these imports were largely armaments. Leopold's relative lack of financial investment resources and his much more acquisitive and short-term exploitative interests hampered the development of a railway and a money economy. To exploit as rapaciously as possible the most easily accessible forms of wealth the area promised – primarily ivory, rubber, and copal – he needed Africans only as a cheap labour force. Consequently, a developed and coherent currency system, substituting for the barter market economy that had been in place long before the appearance of Europeans, was of little importance to him. In effect, the Congo Free State was founded on the blood of a vast force of slave labour.

Estimates for the 'decline' of the native population range from three to six million during the period of Leopold's personal tenancy. He treated the Congo as his personal fiefdom, created by his own efforts. His was the self-declared 'absolute ownership, uncontested, of the Congo and its riches', and in 1906 he asserted:

> The Congo has been, and could have been, nothing but a personal undertaking. There is no more legitimate or respectable right than that of an author over his own work, the fruit of his labour. . . . My rights over the Congo are to be shared with none; they are the fruit of my own struggles and expenditure.[6]

I cite this information partly to offer, however briefly, a historical context for the novel, but also as a way of contextualizing Kurtz and our reading of him. As so much depends on Marlow's (and our) interpretation of Kurtz, critics have not surprisingly devoted time to searching out models Conrad might have used. In their assiduous historical researches both Norman Sherry and Ian Watt have championed the candidature of some half-dozen possibles.[7] With each new candidate, the aim of the undertaking itself, the search for a single model, is revealed to be more problematic. The very proliferation points to a new conclusion: that in his extreme monomania, brutality, and drive for self-aggrandizement, Kurtz is instancing what was an extreme but by no means unique expression of European civilization in its colonizing form. Marlow might be aghast at Kurtz's insane and tormented delusions:

> The wastes of his weary brain were haunted by shadowy images now — images of wealth and fame revolving obsequiously round his un-extinguishable gift of noble and lofty expression. My Intended, my station, my career, my ideas — these were the subjects for the occasional utterances of elevated sentiments. (p. 110)

But Kurtz's discourse starts to look like a model of restrained modesty compared with Leopold's (presumably sane) declaration: 'The King was the founder of the State; he was its organizer, its owner, its absolute sovereign'.[8]

(ii) Conrad's Congo

Conrad spent some six months in the Congo, from June to December 1890 employed by Leopold's Société Anonyme Belge pour le Commerce du Haut-Congo, a business concession in Brussels, headed by Albert Thys with significant funding from British and American financiers. Evidence seems to indicate that Conrad's initial interest was in finding steady employment, and this Africa posting offered itself. Only subsequently were his boyhood interests in the continent rekindled. His fascination was short-lived. His letters and the *Congo Diary* testify to the increasing sense of disillusionment and frustration and the severe physical and mental deterioration and collapse he suffered there. But they also suggest that his disenchantment was personal rather than political. Indeed, it may well be that he *saw* less evidence of brutality and mutilation than he was later to read about in the growing number of official reports and newspaper articles coming out of Central Africa on atrocities and exploitation. But though the sources for the novel's political critique were therefore not just personal experience, *Heart of Darkness* leaves little doubt about Conrad's verdict on Leopold's rule. It was unequivocal. In a letter to his publisher, Blackwood, of 31 December, 1898, outlining the idea of (*The*) *Heart of Darkness*, he talks of 'the criminality of inefficiency and pure selfishness when tackling the civilizing work in Africa',[9] and in one of his last essays he remembers his Congo journey and night time by the Stanley Falls ('the Inner Station'):

> [T]here was no shadowy friend to stand by my side in the night of the enormous wilderness, no great haunting memory, but only the unholy recollection of a prosaic newspaper 'stunt' and the distasteful knowledge of the vilest scramble for loot that ever disfigured the history of human conscience and geographical exploration. What an end to the idealized realities of a boy's daydreams![10]

How is the anger of these experiences translated in their fictionalized form? What signs and traces of colonialism are represented in the work? Answers to these will provoke supplementary questions. What, if anything, do they tell us about Conrad's general stance toward imperialism?

And here's a further issue. I have mentioned some manifestations of a colonizing presence that we should look for: military control, administration, the establishing of lines of communication (especially railways), the exploitation of a native labour force to produce the country's natural resources. Now, if we think about the last of these (slave labour), we should also attend to three of its facets in addition to the obvious one of brutal physical control: detribalization (the removal of natives from their normal environment and habitual social groupings and practices); the imposition of an alien language (necessary for administrative control); and the transformation of indigenous cultural practices and rituals through the introduction of European culture. **Can we find any symptoms in the novel of these effects of colonization? Please review pp. 39–92, considering what evidence you find of a colonizing presence.**

Let us now work through some specific passages in detail, taking first the description of the French man-of-war. What conclusions do you draw from the way Conrad has described it?

Once, I remember we came upon a man-of-war anchored off the coast. There wasn't even a shed there, and she was shelling the bush. It appears the French had one of their wars going on thereabouts. Her ensign dropped limp like a rag; the muzzles of the long six-inch guns stuck out all over the low hull; the greasy, slimy swell swung her up lazily and let her down swaying her thin masts. In the empty immensity of earth, sky, and water, there she was, incomprehensible, firing into a continent. Pop, would go one of the six-inch guns; a small flame would dart and vanish, a little white smoke would disappear, a tiny projectile would give a feeble screech — and nothing happened. Nothing could happen. There was a touch of insanity in the proceeding, a sense of lugubrious drollery in the sight; and it was not dissipated by somebody on board assuring me earnestly there was a camp of natives — he called them enemies! — hidden out of sight somewhere.   (pp. 40–1)

How is the French military presence portrayed? Does it in any way correspond to the novel's earlier renderings of colonial activities — for example, the absurdity of Fresleven's death? How does the passage achieve its effects? Consider, for example, such phrases as 'firing into a continent' and 'a tiny projectile'.

DISCUSSION

Military intervention here is seen primarily by Marlow as incomprehensible and absurd. Again, as with Fresleven, we find a discrepancy between cause and effect, purpose and achievement. How is this realized? A lot has to do with the recurrent emphasis on size and physical disproportion ('little', 'small flame would dart' juxtaposed against 'immensity', 'continent'). And the 'insanity' is made none the less an 'insanity' by its being a brutally regular occurrence ('The French had one of their wars going on thereabouts'), or by the explanation Marlow is offered, with its verbal mendacity to which he draws attention ('natives — he called them enemies!'). Incidentally, the fact that it is a *French* ship seems to widen Conrad's attack; it surely gives us grounds for concluding that his critique has a more general application to other (or all?) European colonial powers. In answer to a Polish correspondent criticizing him for a pro-English bias, Conrad refers to this incident:

> If I say that the ship which bombarded the coast was French, it is simply because she was French. . . . It happened during the war (!) in Dahomey. What follows could refer just as well to a ship of a different country. [11]

In Chapter 3 we considered Marlow's contradictory position as the self-aware and critical but complicit employee of the Company. Now, I think, in his perception of the French man-of-war we can see the positive aspect of his 'distance' from events. As observer and narrator he embraces the role of outsider: in his account, the deconstruction of the action into discrete entities is paralleled by an equivalent unpacking of the rhetoric of conquest. By putting the 'ordinary' occurrence of naval shelling under the microscope of detailed and alienated observation, Marlow 'de-familiarizes' it and releases himself (and the reader) from the unquestioning view of his fellow travellers on board, who would take a statement like 'The French are shelling enemy camps' for granted. His marginality permits a dual – and devastating – perspective.

Another trace of military presence – intimately linked to the establishing of administrative rule – is so fleetingly referred to ('landed more soldiers – to take care of the custom house clerks, presumably') that we might miss its significance. Yet the passage contains a crucial insight of Conrad's into the processes of colonization:

> Some, I heard, got drowned in the surf, but whether they did or not, nobody seemed particularly to care. They were just flung out there, and on we went. (p. 40)

The victims of colonialism are not just the natives who are enslaved and the physical environment that is ravaged, but the victimizers, too, those who are the white instruments of empire-building. Like a destructive machine, once set in action it owes no more allegiance to its creator and agents than to its most obvious victims. Like the old knitters indifferent to Marlow's fate, the colonial machine doesn't particularly seem to care for anything but material gain. With this insight into colonial practice, which was far from the jingoistic sentiments of the sort familiar to readers of *Blackwood's Magazine*, Conrad is allying himself with earlier nineteenth-century works (such as Mary Shelley's *Frankenstein* and Dickens' *Hard Times*) which present critiques of the dialectics of industrial rationalization, and is tracing its extension into the colonizing process.

The image of the French man-of-war has a powerful and precise impact. **Can you notice other examples of this technique of defamiliarization in Marlow's subsequent narrative which involve the suspension of meaning? Do they also exploit the same 'language effect'? Look particularly at the following pages: 42–4, 79–82, 89.**

DISCUSSION

Startling and brutal images demand notice. The chain-gang and the blacks dying in the grove of death greet Marlow as his first encounter with company 'methods'. Later the attack on his boat is so presented as to accentuate, through the tactic of delayed disclosure, the increasing sense of the bizarre and incomprehensible. Marlow sees the poleman 'inexplicably give up the business suddenly and stretch himself flat on the deck' (p. 80); the gesture is dwelt on because it *appears* meaningless – then Marlow realizes they are under attack. The 'foolish' helmsman falls inexplicably at his feet; his feet get warm and wet – from the dying helmsman's blood. And surely most horrific of all is the double-sighting of the posts encircling Kurtz's house, seen first as ornamental carvings, eventually leaping into view as human skulls – graphic and symbolic testimony to Kurtz's lack of 'restraint' (pp. 89, 97). These moments, possibly the most powerfully visualized in the novel, seem to me to share in stark brutality; they share also in a characteristic structure of delayed disclosure. But apart from the initial shock they elicit, do they all provide the *same* effect of understanding?

A general question ultimately is involved here: does this creation of the sense of mystery lead to fuller clarification – or just mystification? I am appalled, yes; but how am I to *understand* them; indeed, are there available terms through which I can? To have a feeling about an event is not the same as to come to comprehend it. If I react with 'How horrific!' or 'How absurd!', 'It's all a muddle', or 'It's an insoluble mystery', I may express my shock or incredulity. But am I any nearer understanding the event? One critical view of Conrad suggests that this is precisely his point – he is wishing to reveal through such examples as I have cited the essential absurdity and meaninglessness of the universe: things do not have clear purposes. According to this view, to seek to comprehend them is therefore futile. Other powerful critical arguments suggest that Conrad engages in mystification through delayed disclosure and the 'adjectival insistence' on obscurity – and criticize him for it.[12] **Do you think the reader's drive for comprehension and meaning is misplaced in the case of Conrad? Or is it justified, but frustrated by Conrad's obscuring language? Consider the following three examples:**

(a) the heads on the stakes (pp. 89, 96).

(b) the look on the dying helmsman's face (p. 82).

(c) the description of the wilderness charming Kurtz's soul by 'the inconceivable ceremonies of some devilish initiation' (p. 84)

All involve some sort of mystery and obscurity. But are the effects the same in each case? Are they mystery or mystification?

DISCUSSION

Perhaps both critical positions – those that confirm chaos and those that condemn Conrad – overlook real contradictory tendencies in

Conrad's work. I want to argue that the technique of defamiliarization and mystification is not exploited in the same way in
all its instances. In (a) (as in the earlier cases of the French warship
and the chain-gang), it seems to me that mystery works as a step
towards greater comprehension, not as an end in itself. And I think
that Marlow comes to understanding (including political understanding, self-understanding) through the experience of distancing.
Indeed, I think the *process* of narration reveals this. The shocking
realization of the monstrous 'normality' of Kurtz's barbarities requires the controlled creation of mystery. However (and I will
elaborate on this in the next chapter), I would agree that Conrad does
on occasion create a sensational effect in some of the later episodes
and remains satisfied with that – a shock or 'inconceivable mystery'
for its own sake. I think (c) exemplifies this; I'm not so sure about (b)
but think it is moving steadily in this mystifying direction.

Let us pursue the argument by looking carefully at the chain-gang
episode. Think about the actual sights Marlow witnesses, but also
about the mode of representation, the narrative position, Marlow
adopts in describing them. What second-order meaning might there
be in the way he tells it? Read again Marlow's description of the
Company station (pp. 42–5).

> I came upon more pieces of decaying machinery, a stack of rusty rails.
> To the left a clump of trees made a shady spot, where dark things
> seemed to stir feebly. I blinked, the path was steep. A horn tooted to
> the right, and I saw the black people run. A heavy and dull detonation
> shook the ground, a puff of smoke came out of the cliff, and that was
> all. No change appeared on the face of the rock. They were building a
> railway. The cliff was not in the way or anything; but this objectless
> blasting was all the work going on.
>   A slight clinking behind me made me turn my head. Six black men
> advanced in a file, toiling up the path. They walked erect and slow,
> balancing small baskets full of earth on their heads, and the clink kept
> time with their footsteps. Black rags were wound round their loins,
> and the short ends behind waggled to and fro like tails. I could see
> every rib, the joints of their limbs were like knots in a rope; each had
> an iron collar on his neck, and all were connected together with a
> chain whose bights swung between them, rhythmically clinking.
> Another report from the cliff made me think suddenly of that ship of
> war I had seen firing into a continent. It was the same kind of ominous
> voice; but these men could by no stretch of imagination be called
> enemies. They were called criminals, and the outraged law, like the
> bursting shells, had come to them, an insoluble mystery from the sea.
> All their meagre breasts panted together, the violently dilated nostrils
> quivered, the eyes stared stonily uphill. They passed me within six
> inches, without a glance, with that complete, deathlike indifference of
> unhappy savages. Behind this raw matter one of the reclaimed, the

product of the new forces at work, strolled despondently, carrying a rifle by its middle. He had a uniform jacket with one button off, and seeing a white man on the path, hoisted his weapon to his shoulder with alacrity. This was simple prudence, white men being so much alike at a distance that he could not tell who I might be. He was speedily reassured, and with a large, white, rascally grin, and a glance at his charge, seemed to take me into partnership in his exalted trust. After all, I also was a part of the great cause of these high and just proceedings.

Although Marlow sees 'they were building a railway' and then witnesses the chain-gang, he does not actually *say* that directly and immediately. In fact he does not use the word 'chain-gang' here at all. **What is the effect of withholding this information? What does Marlow stress? What is the effect of the phrases 'dark things seemed to stir feebly' or 'raw matter'? When, remembering the French destroyer, he repeats the phrase, 'they were called enemies', what point is he making?**

DISCUSSION

Going straight to the details of what he witnesses, Marlow gives us images of appalling decay and futile suffering, waste and physical atrocity, and this is surely accentuated by such brutal phrases as 'raw matter'. But at a second level of meaning, the presentation is almost as startling as its subjects, for the emphasis it allows Conrad to place on Marlow's mode of perception and understanding. The accumulation of particular concrete sense impressions (aural and visual) slowly consolidate into meaning: a horn, people running, a dull detonation . . . 'they were building a railway'. Clinking, advancing blacks, clinking, iron collars . . . a chain-gang. Most atrocious because most physically immediate are surely the descriptions of the 'shapes' in the grove of death. The face, the black bones, the eyelids, the orbs, the bundles of acute angles . . . dying labourers. The barbarous reduction of a whole human being to dislocated parts is a formal protest at the depersonalizing forces of colonialism which cause it, regarding its slaves as disposable matter.

The retarding of the processes of perception, permitting the 'defamiliarization' I've mentioned, acknowledges on a psychologically realistic level Marlow's sense of appalled astonishment. The attention to accumulating detail registers, I think, *Marlow's* (not the Law's!) dawning outrage. But it doesn't rest there. There is a theoretical issue at stake here to do with how we represent things to ourselves, the signifying act of attributing meanings to signs. Besides its psychological justification, the delaying of recognition has the function of holding the sign in suspension, whether the sign is

linguistic or sensory. However momentarily, the signified referent is
withheld. (Marlow hears a clinking – the sign – and only gradually
attributes signification to it: it is the chains of a chain-gang.) In this
way the signifying act itself is held up for scrutiny. For Conrad, this
scrutiny resolves itself into the quite literal question, how are we to
'call' this? 'These men could by no stretch of imagination be called
enemies. They were called criminals, and the outraged law, like the
bursting shells, had come to them, an insoluble mystery from the sea'
(p. 43). To make doubly sure, Conrad, rarely one to use a single word
when two will do just as well, repeats the point.

'They were dying slowly – it was very clear. They were not
enemies, they were not criminals, they were nothing earthly now.'
For Marlow, for Conrad, 'naming', the relating of signs to signifieds,
is not an innocent act. To name is to give a meaning to, and that can
be political. Perhaps his own agonized difficulties in writing and the
fact of his speaking and writing in an acquired language, his third,
lent him, along with disadvantages critics have traced in his style, this
strength. Because it did not come naturally to him, he was more
consciously aware of its snares; in struggling with his own meanings
he became more alert to the dissimulating ease of others' rhetoric.
We might also notice that by now Marlow has linked – that is,
grasped as having a relation to one another – seemingly disparate
and 'mysterious' elements of colonial activity (exploding shells, the
law, and slave labour).

Within the text the perspective of the uninitiated observer
permits Marlow to unpack the politics of these sights by deconstruct-
ing the actions and the language which embody them. An assault on
colonial power is an assault on its language – and vice versa, even
when it takes the form of callous humour. Marlow invokes the
colonial lie that the blacks were not slaves but free men, paid for their
labour, by 'calling' them 'free as air – and nearly as thin' (p. 44).

Here acidic humour channels rather than smothers the power-
less anger. However troubling the conjunction of barbarity and
humour, in this instance the object of the humour is surely the
perpetrators of the barbarity – the white European business interests.

Other activities are similarly demystified by Conrad when he
unpacks the abstracting phrases by which they are justified: '[T]hey
were building a railway', 'the work was going on'. Though he is
clearly thereby identifying the economic inefficiency and waste – the
'absurdity' of the activities – he's doing much more. The absence of a
defined grammatical subject pretends that the processes of 'development' go on independent of human agency. (In the context, 'they' is
impersonalized.) In a sense this is true, seen from the perspective of
political and economic interests in Europe, represented by the aptly

named Société Anonyme. But Conrad wants to give bodies to this subject. The Société Anonyme could talk of a feat of technological progress and economic profitability. Conrad, with however a problematic and romanticized view, takes the fact of 'work' more literally in these pages as the reality of labour. Conrad's attitude coincides here with Brecht's, whose famous poem 'Questions from a Worker who Reads' can express better than I can how this should affect our view of history:[13]

> Who built Thebes of the seven gates?
> In the books you will find the names of kings.
> Did the kings haul up the lumps of rock?
> And Babylon, many times demolished,
> Who raised it up so many times? In what houses
> Of gold-glittering Lima did the builders live?
> Where, the evening that the Wall of China was finished
> Did the masons go? Great Rome
> Is full of triumphal arches. Who erected them? Over whom
> Did the Caesars triumph? Had Byzantium, much praised in song
> Only palaces for its inhabitants? Even in fabled Atlantis
> The night the ocean engulfed it
> The drowning still bawled for their slaves.

(iii) Anti-Colonialist . . . or Colonialist?

Still, the question has to be faced: how specifically *does* Conrad register these human subjects? Does he render them fully and concretely? In a forceful attack on Conrad as 'a bloody racist', the Nigerian novelist Chinua Achebe argues that Conrad is not really interested in Africa or Africans; he uses the country 'as a setting and backdrop which eliminates the African as a human factor . . . as a metaphysical battlefield devoid of all recognizable humanity, into which the wandering European enters at his peril'.[14] I'll consider the full weight of this critique when I come to consider the thematic clash of 'civilization' and 'savagery' in the next chapter. **But do you agree that for all the apparent sympathy Conrad shows for them, his portrayal of these blacks – in the chain-gang, in the groves of death – reveals a dehumanizing indifference to their individuality?**

DISCUSSION

I would agree that they are not personally characterized (in the way that the chief accountant, the fastidious pigeon-loving boiler-maker, the first-class agent are – though perhaps these portraits border on caricature). But in his depiction of his encounters with them, early on in his journey, we are surely given some sense of differentiation, of different histories, however fleeting. Some he recognizes as brutally displaced from their tribal homes: 'Brought from all the recesses of the coast in all the legality of time contracts, lost in uncongenial surroundings, fed on unfamiliar food, they sickened, became inefficient, and were then allowed to crawl away and rest' (p. 44). This, surely, casts the European stereotypes of 'inefficient' and 'listless' blacks in a new light. Later at the Central Station (p. 55), there is a *suggestion* of Africans resisting their enslavement by an act of sabotage (burning the storehouse).

A further and telling portrait of detribalization can be found in the figure of the black overseer to the chain-gang. In 1891 the estimated European population in the 'Congo Free State' was 700 (mostly Belgian). They relied on a force of native militia under white control to organize the system of forced labour both for building work and for the collection of wild rubber and ivory which were the area's major exports. So natives were often placed in positions of authority over others, when they were not already tribal chiefs, and to fulfil work or collection quotas they would frequently resort to coercion and mutilation to encourage output and 'discipline'.

Look again at the description of the chain-gang overseer (p. 43). What does it tell us about black/white relations? And does it reveal anything new about the position Marlow is taking to the sights he is witnessing? What, for example, about the position which, as a white 'observer', he is placing himself in? What is revealed about his relation to the acts perpetrated in the interests of the philanthropic mission?

DISCUSSION

I noted how economically Conrad delineates the guard's contradictory responses: despondency, fear, obsequiousness, and conspiratorial trust, a series of reactions convincingly revealing one version of the complex attitudes of the colonized to colonizer. Equally striking, I suggest, is Marlow's awareness of the contradictions of *his* position. Indeed, I would argue that it is this self-awareness which marks him off so profoundly from all other Europeans in the novel. He has the self-consciousness of one on the margin, which exacerbates his marginality. He has a self-distancing capacity which tries to imagine what it must be like to look at a white if you're not one. I say 'tries to', for there must surely still be something ethnocentric in what Marlow attributes to the guard. As a white man he is still *imputing* a way of looking to the black guard. How can we imagine the 'other' – another person, another culture? By what anthropologists used to call the 'if I were a horse' approach to understanding other cultures?

In the main, the traders, missionaries, and administrators who came to Central Africa did not even imagine 'imagining the other'. In this respect Marlow is different. When he is at his most equine, Marlow tries to imagine. This usually takes the form of acknowledging to himself that Africans pose a question, a mystery – but without (and, I hope to show, this is crucial) either hypostatizing the mystery *as* mystification *or* resolving it through the 'answers' unconsciously provided by white stereotypes. For Marlow, the blacks pose questions potentially explicable within their own terms and norms. For example, Marlow is ready to *ask*, at least, whether the drums he hears in the distance don't have as normal a place in tribal culture, 'as profound a meaning as the sound of bells in a Christian country' (p. 48). Similarly, he asks whether a deserted village would strike us as that odd if we translated the context to a Kentish village between Deal and Gravesend suddenly threatened by the invasion of 'a lot of mysterious niggers armed with all kinds of fearful weapons' (p. 48). The startlingly incongruous white-worsted neckwear on one of the dying 'black shadows' (p. 45) provokes questions which ask for a history, but the questions do not get stereotypic answers involving superstition or fetishism – which other Europeans, who of course never wear crosses or lucky charms, might proffer.

In the specific instance of the black guard, Marlow 'imagines the other' this far: he silently acknowledges one of the stereotypic racist ways in which the 'superior' white man sees the black. We all know that Chinamen look the same. Ditto savage blacks. But us? With our obvious individual differences? Marlow invokes the cliché through ironic inversion: the overseer acts prudently because 'white men being so much alike at a distance that he couldn't tell who I might be'. Think of the discomforting effect, if pursued at length, this way of looking would have on Marlow's listeners. He is conscious enough of some racial stereotypes to turn them ironically against their white users. The irony is also uncomfortably directed therefore against himself – for the guard recognizes (or is it that Marlow projects on to him the recognition?) that Marlow is one of his white bosses, a party to the civilizing mission. And of course Marlow's problem is that he *is*: a small but would-be efficient cog in the wheel of empire.[15]

But at the same time as recognizing his complicity, Marlow tries to walk away from it – literally, taking an easy 'stroll' into the grove of death. Of course he cannot escape it; but neither can he adopt a stable, non-contradictory position towards it. This accounts in part, I think, for what has led critics into contention over whether Conrad (accused of being the author of these contradictions) is a racist or a

debunker of racial myths; a patriotic colonialist (at least if the
Empire is efficient and British) or a virulent critic of colonialism (if it
is not).[16] In a sense these critics are rehearsing and seeking to resolve
unilaterally and at an interpretative level, the contradictions in
Marlow's position which exist at a cultural and political one.

We have already found earlier examples of embarrassed contradiction in Marlow which are pertinent here – the discomfort he feels
in his interviews with the doctor and his aunt (p. 38), which I
discussed in Chapter 3 and which you may want to recall. There I
suggested that in their different ways these incidents reveal an
irritation which could be read as symptoms of the same contradictions: Marlow has difficulty recognizing his complicity, but we can
read it in his behaviour. The point *is not* to say which side of the
racialist/colonialist fence Conrad is coming down on. To do so we
would be denying the real contradiction and complicity in Marlow's
position, which Conrad's text reveals.

Marlow oscillates uneasily in this position. He displays at times a
critical self-consciousness, voiced in demystifying irony and hardly-
veiled anger. At other times he assumes an unconscious attitude of
(class or racial?) superiority, as, for example, when he is offended by
the 'provoking insolence' of the manager's overfed negro 'boy' (p.
51). Most characteristically, he resorts to a willed retreat into the
'ideal' of work and efficiency which represents for him a precarious
kind of 'resolution'. Marlow's recourse to the latter will be examined
subsequently; for the moment let us probe further the function and
also the problematics of his ironic voice.

In an 'Author's Note' introducing *The Secret Agent*, Conrad
talks of his subject as

> the criminal futility of the whole thing, doctrine, action, mentality;
> and on the contemptible aspect of the half-crazy pose as of a brazen
> cheat exploiting the poignant miseries and passionate credulities of a
> mankind always so tragically eager for self-destruction.[17]

It seems uncannily close to Leopold's mad 'adventure' – or Kurtz's
fictional version of it. Significantly, Conrad adds, 'The ironic treatment alone would enable me to say all I felt I would have to say in
scorn as well as pity'. The critical distance from imperial discourse
and action which irony discloses is nowhere more evident than in
Marlow's scorn for the 'papier-mâché Mephistopheles' brickmaker,
the 'hollow' manager and his uncle's devoted band, which, we note,
'called itself' the Eldorado Exploring Expedition. His scathing dismissal of the last can stand for the rest: 'Long afterwards the news
came that all the donkeys were dead. I know nothing as to the fate of
the less valuable animals' (p. 66).

But irony in Conrad's fiction – and perhaps this is true of any fiction – is double-edged. Once the play of irony commences, how can we be sure of its direction and cessation? Can we confidently distinguish between the irony of Marlow's voice which Conrad endorses and an irony emanating from Conrad with Marlow as its object? Further, irony implies normative categories of judgement. How are these securely (that is, non-ironically) invoked? And can an acerbic ironic voice avoid a sort of complicity with what it exposes? We need to consider these more theoretical implications of irony before trying to judge its range in *Heart of Darkness*. It seems to me that irony is characteristically generated by and produces critical distancing. It often aims at recognition and understanding through mock-callous indifference. But is it then not precisely analogous to the 'scorn', the dehumanizing objectification of the human, which, as a way of looking at the world, has permitted the very exploitation the irony targets? Irony fends off the horror of the experience by deflecting it into the self-protective form of the sardonic, the cynical, or the bizarre. But it may thereby re-enact the culpable processes it is at base criticizing. Do you think Marlow altogether avoids this double-bind?

As to the direction of irony, let us look by way of example at the description of the African fireman aboard Marlow's steamer:

And between whiles I had to look after the savage who was fireman. He was an improved specimen; he could fire up a vertical boiler. He was there below me, and, upon my word, to look at him was as edifying as seeing a dog in a parody of breeches and a feather hat, walking on his hind-legs. A few months of training had done for that really fine chap. He squinted at the steam-gauge and at the water-gauge with an evident effort of intrepidity – and he had filed teeth, too, the poor devil, and the wool of his pate shaved into queer patterns, and three ornamental scars on each of his cheeks. He ought to have been clapping his hands and stamping his feet on the bank, instead of which he was hard at work, a thrall to strange witchcraft, full of improving knowledge. He was useful because he had been instructed; and what he knew was this – that should the water in that transparent thing disappear, the evil spirit inside the boiler would get angry through the greatness of his thirst, and take a terrible vengeance. So he sweated and fired up and watched the glass fearfully (with an impromptu charm, made of rags, tied to his arm, and a piece of polished bone, as big as a watch, stuck flatways through his lower lip), while the wooded banks slipped past us slowly, the short noise was left behind, the interminable miles of silence – and we crept on, towards Kurtz. But the snags were thick, the water was treacherous and shallow, the boiler seemed indeed to have a sulky devil in it, and thus neither that fireman nor I had any time to peer into our creepy thoughts.   (p. 70)

How do you read this?
Here is Achebe's view of the passage:

> Having shown us Africa in the mass, Conrad then zeros in on a specific example, giving us one of his rare descriptions of an African who is not just limbs or rolling eyes:
>   (*he quotes from the passage*)
> As everybody knows, Conrad is a romantic on the side. He might not exactly admire savages clapping their hands and stamping their feet but they have at least the merit of being in their place, unlike this dog in a parody of breeches. For Conrad, things (and persons) being in their place is of the utmost importance.[18]

Do you find Achebe's reading persuasive? Is Marlow mocking the 'dog in a parody of breeches'? What tone do you discern in 'improved specimen' and 'really fine chap'? Is Marlow unwittingly giving more evidence of his (Conrad's?) assumptions of racial superiority? Or is his irony directed elsewhere?

DISCUSSION

In one way I think Achebe is right, but not wholly in the sense he means. He says that for Conrad things should be in their place, and he goes on to imply that Conrad evokes ethnocentric racial stereotypes of savages stamping about, to define where that place is. But if we take Conrad's ideas of 'right place' and 'displacement' more dialectically, can we not also recognize their positive thrust? We might recall almost the only unambiguously lyrical passage in the whole work, the description of the blacks riding the surf, which significantly comes directly before and is juxtaposed to that of the French destroyer (p. 40).

> The voice of the surf now and then was a positive pleasure, like the speech of a brother. It was something natural, that had its reason, that had a meaning. Now and then a boat from the shore gave one a momentary contact with reality. It was paddled by black fellows. You could see from afar the white of their eyeballs glistening. They shouted, sang; their bodies streamed with perspiration; they had faces like grotesque masks – these chaps; but they had bone, muscle, a wild vitality, an intense energy of movement, that was as natural and true as the surf along their coast. They wanted no excuse for being there. They were a great comfort to look at. For a time I would feel I belonged still to a world of straight-forward facts; but the feeling would not last long. Something would turn up to scare it away.

It is a rare moment of immediately affirmed meaning and harmony, against which we can measure the various degrees and forms of displacement Marlow subsequently experiences.

Set against that, the fireman *is* 'out of place.' We do not have to deny or condone the stereotyping of dancing savages to agree with *that*. And who else is 'out of place'? Surely the Europeans who have come with their 'strange witchcraft' and displaced him, sought to detribalize him. I think the irony increasingly turns against those who have chosen to put themselves in the wrong place, bringing their 'improving knowledge', their 'instruction', which mystifies and fetishizes their 'superior' technology. If the description starts with Marlow at an ironic distance from the 'improved specimen' (echoes of the doctor's discourse) it ends with him placing himself in close alliance with the fireman, for all their difference. For with their work 'neither that fireman nor I had any time to peer into our creepy thoughts'. The direction of the irony, in other words, is never stable.

We meet here a central critical problem in our reading of Conrad (indeed of any ironic text), one that Achebe's argument brilliantly highlights: what is Conrad's attitude to Marlow and ours to Conrad? When is he endorsing Marlow and when exposing him to irony? The embedding of Marlow's narrative within the anonymous first person's makes it impossible for the reader to identify a controlling Conradian 'meta-discourse' which might offer an arbitrating (alternative) frame of critical reference. This is how Achebe puts it:

> [If] Conrad's intention is to draw a *cordon sanitaire* between himself and the moral and psychological malaise of his narrator, his care seems to me totally wasted because he neglects to hint however subtly or tentatively at an alternative frame of reference by which we may judge the actions and opinions of his characters.[19]

He concludes that 'Marlow seems . . . to enjoy Conrad's complete confidence'. Is this conclusion one that we, too, must draw?

F. R. Leavis argues for a close identification of Conrad and Marlow, but values this quite differently:

> Conrad, for all his sophistication, exhibits a certain simplicity of outlook and attitude . . . something of the gallant simple sailor.
> The sailor in him, of course, is rightly held to be a main part of his strength. It is not for nothing that *Heart of Darkness*, a predominantly successful tale, is told by the captain of the steamboat – told from that specific and concretely realized point of view.[20]

Both Achebe and Leavis share the view that Marlow must be identified with Conrad, Achebe regretfully and Leavis with positive endorsement. Lying behind Leavis's position is what he takes as Marlow's moral virtue, embodied in his commitment to work. Can work then represent a standard for the moral judgement of action and a basis for the discrimination of ironies (something which Achebe also seeks, but in vain)?

(iv) The Idea of Work

This has become a central issue for critics. What *is* Marlow's attitude
to work? And does this provide a coherent norm of judgement which
the text endorses? You might recall earlier references to 'efficiency'
(p. 31) and 'real work' (p. 36). **Now consider the depictions of the
'devoted band' of the Eldorado Expedition (pp. 61, 66), the fireman
(p. 70), and the chain-gang. Does efficiency of work prove the basis
by which Marlow judges them? And do you find this adequate?**

DISCUSSION

It does seem to me that purposive and efficient donkey-work is a
moral positive for Marlow. So let us consider further the 'equine'.
The donkeys (unlike the devoted band) are valuable because they do
a practical job of work. This motif echoes the earlier one: the 'vast
amount of red' on the map in the Director's office, so comforting to
Marlow because he knows 'some real work is done in there' (p. 36).
The capacity for conscientious − if unself-conscious − labour is
recurrently evoked as the measure of man. The full significance of
this for Marlow's self-understanding will be explored later. But as a
bench-mark for his irony (and thus the enabling presupposition for
his critique of colonial practice), it seems fairly consistent and
plausible. 'Work', 'efficiency', and 'method' are the valorizing terms
against which the futility, wastage, and exploitation he witnesses are
condemned. Marlow is alert to, and his anger has alerted us to, the
stereotypes and ideological pretences justifying the civilizing
mission. Think of his disgust, for example, at the manager's criticism
of Kurtz for his 'unsound method' which was jeopardizing the company's trade interests. 'No method at all', Marlow retorts with
contempt (p. 102).

But as readers we need to question these categories of judgement. If 'the horror' he depicts is to be translated as 'wastage', does
his protest amount simply to an attack on what Conrad also called
'the criminality of inefficiency'? Are we to infer that colonial exploitation and the extremes of Kurtz's behaviour would have been all
right in Marlow's (and Conrad's) eyes if pursued purposefully
and efficiently? Do you think Conrad wants to endorse British
colonialists for their work-ethic?

The idea that efficient work might have redeeming power has
already been offered to us at the outset of the tale:

Mind, none of us would feel exactly like this. What saves us is
efficiency − the devotion to efficiency. . . . What redeems [the conquest of the earth] is the idea only. An idea at the back of it.   (pp.
31–2)

Does Marlow now take efficiency to legitimize territorial conquest? 'I don't like work – no man does – but I like what is in the work – the chance to find yourself', Marlow says (p. 59). Is that colonialism's redeeming virtue? Efficiency?

Consider in this respect the presentation of the chief accountant (pp. 45–6).

DISCUSSION

In one of the work's most telling juxtapositions Marlow rushes from the horrors of the grove of death to the Central Station, where he meets a white man 'in such an unexpected elegance of get-up that in the first moment I took him for a vision' (p. 45). This is the Company's chief accountant, who epitomizes an almost insane insistence on one version of 'civilization' – intended, no doubt, at least on first sight, to appeal to the stiff-upper-lip stereotypes of the tale's audience. 'His appearance was certainly that of a hair-dresser's dummy; but in the great demoralization of the land he kept up his appearance. That's backbone.' Marlow respects his very insistence on propriety and sartorial elegance.

> This man had verily accomplished something. And he was devoted to his books, which were in apple-pie order.
> Everywhere else in the station was in a muddle.   (p. 46)

Genocide, too, needs its bureaucrats. Cool indifference and professional efficiency are registered as bizarre, as a 'miracle', in such a place. But why see them thus as contradictory? They could be thought of as job requirements.

Have we, via Marlow and in the absence of a meta-lingual 'authoritative denial', co-opted Conrad as an enlightened liberal spokesperson for anti-colonialism, only to find ourselves blindly endorsing well-administered death camps? (They got the trains to run on time. Best not ask where to).

Achebe's critique of Conrad's narrative self-effacement, quoted just now, seems compelling. **If we acknowledge Marlow's capacity to evoke cultural stereotypes and ideological myths to demystify them, aren't we stuck with those he appears to leave intact? And in default of a counter-voice, doesn't Conrad, too, expose himself?**

DISCUSSION

To counter Achebe, the way to proceed might be to try to establish Conrad's voice from outside the work, and look to other essays and letters to seek a coherent and consistent position on imperialism.

Here too we meet problems. First, the evidence is contradictory. In the context of the Boer dispute, we can find Conrad in his letters talking proudly, as a British adoptee, of the 'liberty, which can only be found under the English flag'. But other letters find him outspokenly *critical* of British espoused motives: 'There is an appalling futility in this business. If I am to believe Kipling this is a war undertaken for the cause of democracy. C'est à crever de rire'.[21] In other words, to try to ascertain a stable position for Conrad (to differentiate him from Marlow), I have to resort to other *texts* which still are contradictory, still require interpretation. They too engender a plural reading, resisting authoritative closure.

Secondly, what if we *did* find that Conrad's other statements unequivocally endorsed the view that efficiency is the measure of political legitimation, and inefficiency *the* great crime of colonists? If the text itself seems more problematic, more contradictory in its assertions, why as a critical reader should I want to settle that contradiction by attributing a higher truth-status to Conrad's extra-textual pronouncements to achieve an albeit morally disturbing closure?

But I think a different way of engaging Achebe's criticism is to look to the work itself, and in so doing question the notion that it would only be through a meta-lingual counter-discourse (say, the judgements of an omniscient narrator) that we could identify an ironizing commentary on Marlow within the text. For the written work itself, the actions it narrates, can provide a critical context within which we can assess Marlow's judgements. True, all the events of the tale are narrated by Marlow and filtered through the anonymous 'I'. But Marlow is not creator of the (fictional) world he describes. Conrad can still organize the structure of and actions in that world in a way which can comment on Marlow's construing of it. The work will always say more than its narrator will or can explicitly tell. A discourse of actions can supply a critical viewpoint on Marlow's discourse of language. And in a work where 'eloquence' – the rhetoric of civilizing Europe, the rhetoric of Kurtz's report – has become a dirty word, action can speak louder than words. **How does Conrad juxtapose Marlow's seemingly blind *praise* of the 'miracle of efficiency' with what the narrative action then causes him to *see*? Look again at the presentation of the accountant and his actions.**

DISCUSSION

There may be no explicit qualification of the 'miracle of efficiency', but Marlow goes on immediately to record without comment the accountant's annoyance at the groans of an invalided agent which 'distract [his] attention'. The last view Marlow allows us of him is: 'turned to his work . . . bent over his books, [he] was making correct entries of perfectly correct transactions; and fifty feet below the doorstep I could see the still treetops of the grove of death'. There is a necessary political connection between the two clauses (or rather what they refer to). The semi-colon, a sign of the written text, not spoken narration, is a precise notation of Marlow's relation to both sides of the colonial coin: it insists upon a connection without dictating the precise nature of it. Standing in the doorway, Marlow mediates between the two faces of colonialism. He can see – and thus mediate to his audience – the link which the accountant cannot see, and which his statistics, dying in the grove, are perhaps beyond seeing now. It is a perfect physical figure to represent Marlow's own hovering between the administrator and the barbarity he perpetuates. Marlow's semi-colonialism, so to speak, does not fully resolve the contradictions of his position. But it is the text's registering of it which allows us to see them.

Such narrative juxtapositions can be seen as Conrad's way of placing Marlow, and ironically commenting on his cult of efficiency. They also disclose to Marlow's listeners and Conrad's readers an important fact about Kurtz and how we should read *him*. He is not a unique perversion of the European civilizing mission; rather he can be seen as its epitome. Conrad insists upon Kurtz's cosmopolitan representativeness. 'All Europe contributed to the making of Kurtz' and he had all the benefits of Englishmen and Frenchmen among his forebears. To nurture his cultural values 'the original Kurtz had been educated partly in England, and . . . his sympathies were in the right place' (p. 86). The upshot of this cultural heritage could hardly have been more chillingly recorded than in the scrawled footnote of Kurtz's report on the Suppression of Savage Customs. This 'beautiful piece of writing' concludes with the forthright injunction, 'Exterminate all the brutes!' (pp. 86–7). It incorporates the same contradictions of the civilizing will as the miraculous chief accountant and his efficient book-keeping. Opposition to Kurtz within the Company comes because he's seen as a successful rival, not an immoral renegade; his development is the 'logical' extension, not the renunciation, of its practices.

While Conrad was no Marxist – as indeed his energetic exchanges with his socialist friend Cunninghame Graham show[22] – he'd seen and experienced in Poland and Africa enough of the workings of varieties of European imperialism to make him a historical materialist in Walter Benjamin's sense:

And all rulers are the heirs of those who conquered before them. Hence, empathy with the victor invariably benefits the rulers. Historical materialists know what that means. Whoever has emerged victorious participates to this day in the triumphal procession in which the present rulers step over those who are lying prostrate. According to traditional practice, the spoils are carried along in the procession. They are called cultural treasures, and a historical materialist views them with cautious detachment. For without exception the cultural treasures he surveys have an origin which he cannot contemplate without horror. They owe their existence not only to the efforts of the great minds and talents who have created them, but also to the anonymous toil of their contemporaries. There is no document of civilization which is not at the same time a document of barbarism.[23]

To summarize this chapter: I have tried to show how the work can and should be read within, and be seen to register, the historical realities of African colonization. Marlow's particular role is to offer a radical critique of these processes while at the same time revealing the contradictions in his own status. The primary *formal* techniques Conrad employs – of delayed revelation and ironic comment – carry their own benefits in the devastating criticism of the brutalities of colonization and how these actions are normally seen and represented. But they also carry disadvantages. The mystery of the subject sometimes seems like mystification. And the basis for the critique of colonial presence seems to resolve itself at times into the measure of efficiency. But the text finally rests with the displaying (not resolving) of contradictions – epitomized in Marlow's semi-colonialism. The next chapter will investigate a new dimension of this colonialism: the confrontation of 'civilization' and 'the savage'.

5. 'Civilization' and 'Savagery': Marlow Imagining the Other

Marlow the semi-colonialist, Marlow the critical if marginalized observer: I have emphasized these constructions of Marlow to develop the argument in Chapter 2 that they identify a powerful stylistic and thematic structure in the novel. Through Marlow's sceptical, idiosyncratic voice, Conrad is offering a counter-narrative to that of the framing narrator. The latter, who claims to speak normatively for a collective 'us', in fact prepares the reader for a different narrative. But the stereotypic connotations of his discourse ('civilized', 'glorious', 'light/dark') are questioned, if not fully contested, by Marlow's. In the last chapter we saw how Marlow, confronted by the immediacy of bizarre and shocking sights, consciously evokes the rhetoric of colonial practice in order to contrast it with the representation of its realities – even if, when he does so, the narrative further exposes the contradictions of his own position.

But this political-historical interpretation of Marlow's character (as critical outsider) and his narrative function (as providing a rhetorical and thus political critique of colonialism) may, like his boat, hit some snags. You may have been thinking of some already. The following strike me as potential ones. **Consider how much weight you would give them.**

1 This 'semicolonial' reading may be persuasive for part of the book – say, until the up-river journey to Kurtz. But can it be persistently maintained after that? Are there any later incidents or passages in the novel which confirm it?

2 Is Marlow's satirical tone and the criticism it articulates sustained? Do the descriptions of the wilderness or Kurtz's final struggle, for example, register this acerbic attitude?

3 And what of Kurtz? Does the account I have offered of him within

the framework of a political critique correspond to the centrality of his role in the novel? Does it place too much emphasis on Marlow as a central focus of interpretation, whereas, surely, Kurtz is the one we (like Marlow) want to get to and comprehend?

4 And the characterization of Marlow as critical (albeit compromised) observer of colonial practice: does he identify himself consistently in his narrative as this sort of 'outsider'? And do we agree with his self-representation? Who does he align himself with – the 'Pilgrims' and the blacks on board ship, Kurtz, or the inhabitants of the sepulchral city on his return?

DISCUSSION

Some of the questions these snags raise are very broad-ranging. But let me offer some initial responses.

To the first objection, it does indeed seem to me that this political interpretation applies more obviously to earlier portions of the narrative. It's hard to say exactly where a shift away from explicitly political concerns occurs, for there is not, of course, an abrupt discontinuity, but rather a gradual displacement. I would suggest, though, that Marlow's account of starting up-river from the Central Station marks its threshold (p. 66).

I *can* think of later episodes where his barely-muted anger at the maltreatment of blacks and at other extreme expressions of colonial presence surfaces: his response to the manager's talk of Kurtz's 'unsound method' of 'trading', for example (look at p. 102), or his outrage at the Russian Harlequin's description of the heads on the stakes surrounding Kurtz's house (p. 98). But by and large I would agree that incidents registering Marlow's revulsion at the cruelty and apparent absurdity of colonial practice do predominate early on and decline in their frequency and impact in the course of the narrative.

And with it – to take up the second objection – there does, too, seem to me to be a shift in Marlow's narrative tone. As he draws closer to Kurtz – and I mean Kurtz both as the object of his journey and the subject of his narrative – I think Marlow's sardonic voice does get tempered. His hardly-suppressed acerbity at colonial self-interest and complacency is gradually displaced by a tone of contemplative introspection, a 'metaphysical' rather than political self-questioning. Thinking back over the novel as a whole, would you agree with my impression? Contrast the scathing tone through which Marlow registers the stark brutality of the chain-gang with the equally striking but quite different tone in his descriptions of his up-river journey and his account of Kurtz's struggle with the call of the wilderness (pp. 66, 106). The oppressive gloom and psychic threat embodied in these latter descriptions seem to take us a long way from the powerful colonial critique of his earlier discourse. Can a political/historical account of the novel accommodate this shift of emphasis?

And what about the function of Kurtz in the narrative? As Marlow approaches him, does he perceive Kurtz differently from his earlier formulations of him? And do we share this shift in view? You will remember from Chapter 4 that one reading of the novel casts Kurtz as the epitome of colonial excess. I suggested that the narrative implicitly invites us to regard Kurtz and his megalomaniac drive to appropriate the 'dark continent' as representative of the European colonizer. But as Marlow's narrative focuses inexorably on his meeting with Kurtz and its ultimate aftermath – Marlow's lie to Kurtz's Intended – we should be asking ourselves whether we think this reading of Kurtz as a colonizer remains a stable one. And suppose it does not: suppose I saw Kurtz as an aberrant renegade from the European norm rather than as its culmination. What would be the narrative and political implications of that? Would he be more heroic, rising above the mediocrity of the other Europeans? Or would such a reading be more politically complacent, implying that most colonizers aren't as bad as Kurtz? Perhaps neither reading is comfortable. ·

But whichever way we read Kurtz, can we reasonably argue for his narrative *centrality*? I can see that the classic structure of the narrative – the search and rescue of a beleaguered figure – might encourage us into seeing Kurtz as the central narrative 'key'. But, as the idea of such a 'key' has been questioned from the opening description of Marlow's story-telling, Kurtz's narrative function may be equally problematic.

You may have come up with other snags and produced your own arguments and evidence in negotiating them. Whatever responses your reading has produced, you should have been noticing that in the process you, like me, have been arbitrating (or hesitating) between a series of differing 'readings'. For example, you've been deciding on competing readings of Marlow's tone (bitter? indifferent? callous?) and of Kurtz ('universal genius'? 'choice of nightmares'? a 'first-class agent'?).

But what's true of characters is also true of other descriptions. Sometimes you have been reading 'readings' when you may not have been aware of it – rather thinking of them as 'mere' description of the body or of landscape without further interpretative implication. But as Marlow in his 'critique of language' has already demonstrated, 'description' is never neutral; it embodies more or less conscious choices about ways of seeing. (As Kafka precisely put it in writing of one of his characters in *The Castle*, 'Her hands were certainly small and delicate, but they could quite as well have been called weak and characterless'.[1] So while this play of readings is open, our decisions, our interpretations, however provisional, carry implications.

Indeed, the chief argumentative thrust of these objections to the novel as colonial critique is that it prioritizes some elements in the text at the expense of others. And if this is so, is the novel as colonial critique any less reductive or one-sided a reading than we perhaps earlier found a psychological or mythical one to be? And, if I acknowledge shifts of emphasis in the novel's thematic and stylistic features (after, roughly, p. 66), do I henceforth need to abandon completely the political and historically oriented reading? Do I then need to favour, rather, a reading that can accommodate more adequately Marlow's increasing preoccupation with questions of a more 'metaphysical' and interior sort – the nature of 'the mind of man' and 'truth stripped of its cloak of time' (p. 69)? Does the European colonial encounter with Africa and Africans give way to civilized man's deeper encounter with himself? Should politics and history be shed in favour of the more profound – let us get to the essence of things – the more philosophical?

On the contrary, we surely need to see that these alleged oppositions (political vs. philosophical) are highly tendentious. Why assume that the 'philosophical' has no 'political' significance? If the narrative seems to shift from one to the other, we should try to apply some of the insights of the colonial critique at this new level. We have noticed that Marlow's own African experience has exposed him to two interdependent spheres of colonial practice, both to do with differential power and appropriation. And both are profoundly political and historical. The first is the actual physical reality of imperial presence and material exploitation. The second is the way this reality is represented and thought about, the various discourses through which it is organized and understood: the voice of the Law ('criminals'), of military power ('rebels'), of commerce (that 'noble enterprise'), and of science (the Company doctor, the map-maker). At times Marlow has consciously and sceptically come to question not just the 'content' of colonial practice (what this power is doing), but these modes of representing its practice – how it is understood and talked about.

If the political and historical is understood only as 'content', then these elements might diminish in importance as Marlow approaches Kurtz. But what of the other prong of the critique – 'language'? Can the political insights of that still be applied? We need to consider how Marlow talks about the seemingly non-political, non-historical experience of his encounter with Kurtz, to consider the politics of his mode of representation of the latter's 'dark night of the soul'. In this way we can use Marlow's insights to cast a critical light on his own representational practice; we can read Marlow against the grain, to interrogate his readings and the historical/ cultural assumptions that underpin them, trying to extend a linguistic vigilance (which he at times has exercised) to his own discourse.

(i) The Return to the 'Prehistoric'

A good place to start this interrogation is with Marlow's account of his up-river journey from the Central Station to Kurtz, with what I called a threshold (referring to a shift at about p. 66). Here, I suggested, we can discern evidence of a change in Marlow's tone and preoccupations; we are introduced to new perspectives on his way of looking at the world around him. Also, insofar as it provides the immediate narrative (and physical) environment for the appearance of Kurtz himself, the description prepares the reader with a telling context for her or his understanding of Kurtz and what Marlow makes of him.

First, to clear the ground, some general features of the account. **Reread from p. 66 to the appearance of Kurtz, and consider the following questions:**
1 How long does the journey to Kurtz take?
2 How much text-time (or, more precisely, thinking of the number of pages devoted to any particular narrated event, text 'space') does it take before Kurtz actually makes his appearance in the narrative? How much text-time is that since Marlow records arriving at Kurtz's station?
3 How many people does Marlow have contact with?
4 How much is made, in the narrative, of these contacts?
5 What significant action occurs during this time?

DISCUSSION

I came up with the following responses.

1 Marlow tells us the journey took some two months.
2 Marlow records actually seeing Kurtz for the first time on page 99, ten pages after he's recorded landing at the station, the interval being taken up by Marlow's narration of the conversation with the Russian Harlequin. And when Kurtz *does* take centre stage, he is on it for a bare twelve pages. Odd, considering his 'centrality'.
3 This one is a little vaguer. We are told of three or four hardly identified 'pilgrims' and the manager (p. 67); thirty black crew-

men characterized as 'cannibals'; the fireman (p. 70) and foolish helmsman (p. 79); an undetermined number of (unindividuated) white men in settlements (p. 67) and 'savages in the bush': and the Russian Harlequin. Once at Kurtz's station we may add Kurtz's black 'mistress'.

4 To say that Marlow 'had contact' with them is to exaggerate. The narrator, with one or two exceptions, hardly elaborates.

5 Apart from the navigation of the boat, these actions occur: Marlow's finding of Towson's (or Towser's) book, cryptically inscribed; the natives' attack and the death of the helmsman; the long conversation (pp. 90–9) with the Russian Harlequin.

What do these features add up to? Consider your responses to 1 and 3. How much is made of the narrative possibilities of extended social contact? Do you think the action impels you as a reader towards Kurtz?

DISCUSSION

Considering the potentialities, social human engagement is positively eschewed in the narrative. There is virtually no specific characterization, compared to the incisive thumb-nail portraits of, for example, the Chief Accountant or the pigeon-loving foreman earlier on. Despite the time he's with them (in twenty-five pages devoted to the narrative of the trip) and despite their number, the blacks on board ship are, with the exception of the fireman and helmsman, seen as an undifferentiated mass, not as individual participants in any 'social community' of the boat.

Another related feature is speech – or rather the lack of it. Dialogic exchange – an important form of social action which can also create a sense of narrative pace and immediacy – is radically reduced. Marlow is as shut off from his fellow travellers and crew as the boat seems to be from social (and therefore political) contact with those who inhabit the shore. At the same time the ironic tone, which has hitherto been occasioned by such contacts and confrontations, subsides into a more contemplative inward one. From recording, in their stark immediacy, the situations in which he feels bewilderingly complicit, his narrative is now turning to emphasize Marlow's meditation on what he sees. His social isolation on the boat and the boat's relative disengagement from the life on the banks it passes (except as that's perceived in a very telling and characteristic way) create a modified, distanced, and generalizing perspective within which Marlow frames and seeks to understand his experience. Put bluntly, Marlow starts to 'philosophize'. Hence the displacement of

attention away from the explicits of colonial contact. But displacement onto what? Kurtz? If so, wouldn't we get to him all the quicker?
Do we? My sense is that we do not. The narrative action does not
impel us towards Kurtz, but rather defers his appearance. All the
actions are digressions from, even obstacles to, Marlow's meeting
with Kurtz. However much Marlow's explicit and growing fascination for Kurtz impels us towards him, in fact the narrative delays and
deflects this centering on him. The eschewing of the immediately
social and political does not, in other words, seem to be in the
interests of accelerating the presence or foregrounding of Kurtz. He
is the subject of lengthy speculation and rumour. But his significance
seems to lie as much in his absence as in his actual presence, which is
constantly withheld.

One explanation of these shifts could be that they somehow correspond to the 'objective' changes in the land that Conrad was
travelling through, and Marlow's narrative reflects that. To help you
consider this, read the following extracts from biographical studies
of Conrad, which, having established all the historical evidence,
describe the Congo River as Conrad would have seen it in August
and September 1890.

Norman Sherry offers this account:

> Disentangling fact from fiction in the actual journey up-river, we are
> left [from the evidence] with a routine, highly organized venture along
> a fairly frequented riverway linking quite numerous settlements of
> trading posts and factories, and with a number of competent and busy
> men on board, and with Conrad there to learn the route under the
> guidance of a skilled captain.[2]

Another biographer, Z. Najder, contests some of Sherry's points.
(Biographies no less than fictional narratives are subject to disputes
and interpretations.) But he confirms the impression of Stanley Falls,
the 'model' for Kurtz's Inner Station. Stanley Falls

> was then an important government station and a district administra-
> tive centre. It was there that the representative of the government of
> the Congo Free State lived, and a military detachment was stationed
> under the command of a white second lieutenant; there were many
> administration buildings and trade agencies, warehouses with ivory,
> and so forth. Stanley Falls represented a strategic point not only as the
> last town in the upper part of the river that could be reached by
> steamers, but chiefly because of its significant role in the long-lasting
> conflict between the Arabs and the Belgians . . .
>   In place of romance and adventure [Conrad] found ruthless com-
> petition for trade and power, and an organization bent on making
> quick, huge profits. In place of primordial vegetation, he found a
> landscape where the jungle, exploding with succulent foliage,

contrasted grotesquely with the angular elements of imported architecture. All those European buildings that were a source of pride to the local whites must have given him the impression of façades incongruously superimposed upon the omnipresent density of tropical nature. Even the small misshapen steamer, oozing smoke and shaking and croaking, could be taken for a symbol of the repellent, albeit profitable, European penetration.[3]

Now fiction is not subject to any documentary, empirical imperative. These are not standard or 'accurate' accounts against which we assess Conrad's work. But we can still consider how the fictional 'realizations' they may have generated compare to the one before us. **How, then, do these accounts correspond (or fail to correspond) to the narrative of the journey to the Inner Station as Marlow renders it? What is highlighted? What is underemphasized? What do you notice particularly about Marlow's social contacts in relation to what you might have expected from reading the biographical accounts? And how does the portrayal of Kurtz's encampment compare to Stanley Falls?**

DISCUSSION

I noted the following differences:

1 The biographies suggest an active social world in the river-side settlements where native and colonial commercial activities were pursued. The fictional account really downplays this, as it does the impression of a quite populated shore.

2 The way the population on shore is presented by Marlow is emphatic and connotatively potent. For him, the natives – when represented at all – are seen as a single mass of savages, engaged in incomprehensible ritual or combative behaviour, not at all as engaged in daily routines.

3 Kurtz's settlement is much more dilapidated, decaying, and isolated than I'd imagine from Sherry's or Najder's account of Stanley Falls.

4 Kurtz is depicted as a virtually solitary white man who, apart from the Russian Harlequin, is surrounded by a group of disciple blacks. This bears no correspondence to the realities of Stanley Falls.

The fiction, in short, accentuates isolation, white solitariness in the wilderness, and black 'savage' mystery.

Now here's another account, a typical entry from Conrad's 'Up-River Book' of his journey towards Stanley Falls.

Keep a little nearer to the middle island than to the islands on your Port side. Proceeding cautiously must feel your way in 12 to 8 feet water. The shore on the port side is the North Bank of the river.

Snags along but not much off. After passing two little islands you sight a dead trunk of a tree and villages begin. In many places cut bank. Excellent wooding places up to the point and in the great bend. (10h50) Left 11:30 Rounding the 1st point after the dead tree you open the 2nd point bearing ab[ou]t NE where this reach ends. To Starb[oar]d several islands of which two are prominent. Land backing there in a semicircle at a great distance – M[ai]n-Land on the S[ou]th Bank not visible.

The river very broad here. Follow close in the bend as there is a large sandbank between the island and the main shore.

Nearing the P[oin]t sounding in 12 to 10 feet (at 1/2 F.W.)

Mind a very bad snag nearly off the point. After a bit of straight shore and a small point ab[ou]t ENE open out 2 small islets come in sight. Steer along the m[ai]n shore. When pass[in]g the islets much caution and good look out – sandbanks.[4]

Does this tally in any way with Marlow's narrative? Think particularly of the implied attitude to the physical surroundings.

DISCUSSION

The similarities I noted between Marlow's account and that in Conrad's *Congo Diary* include:

1 a preoccupation with navigational difficulties.
2 an atmosphere of cautious tension betrayed by an exhausting vigilance. (Note the concern with orientation, supplies of wood, and 'points'.)
3 no reference to or contact with life on shore – despite mention of populated villages. Both accounts underline an ignorance of and isolation from the activities of land-dwellers.

So one aspect of the fictional narrative *is* highlighted – Marlow's alertness to the mechanics and dangers of steering the boat. Indeed, the immediate factual reference to features and hazards of river and shore in Conrad's log-book detail and underline the sense of physical struggle and danger that Marlow experiences. But even as I suggest these similarities, I realize differences, too, and notice what is really absent from the journal: descriptions of the surrounding jungle. What references there are to the land reduce it to the concretely physical and answer to the need for supplies of wood and so on. The landscape as imaginatively contemplated by Marlow has no place in Conrad's workmanlike prose. Careful steering for Conrad is a fact of professional life. For Marlow it is that – but it is made to stand for much more. Its dangers and demands bear a significant relation to the dangers (and demands) of the other space, the wilderness and what it harbours.

Look carefully again at the following passage. **What does it imply about the role of physical work?** You might also recall the discussion in Chapter 4 of the 'redeeming value' of work and Marlow's pleasure at seeing red on the map of Africa, where he knew 'real work was going on'. **Is this the sort of work Marlow means? What is his attitude towards it now?**

> You wonder I didn't go ashore for a howl and a dance? Well, no – I didn't. Fine sentiments, you say? Fine sentiments, be hanged! I had no time. I had to mess about with white-lead and strips of woollen blanket helping to put bandages on those leaky steampipes – I tell you. I had to watch the steering, and circumvent those snags, and get the tin-pot along by hook or by crook. There was surface-truth enough in these things to save a wiser man.   (pp. 69–70)

DISCUSSION

The value Marlow sees in work here lies surely not in the concrete products of it (more ivory, more wealth), but in its side-products; in its psychological rather than material function. Remember what Marlow has said of work: 'I don't like work – no man does – but I like what is in the work – the chance to find yourself' (p. 59). So work is a source of self-discovery. But now this discovery takes a para-doxical if not contradictory form. Here, the psychological function of work is as a self-defence against fearsome self-awareness. Work is a personal 'surface-truth' which protects you from knowing yourself.

So over and above the immediate purpose of work – getting the ship along – and at the same time as emphasizing its inherent risks, labour functions to stave off a far bigger, less concrete thought, the thought of what the jungle means to Marlow. He displaces that threat through labour. Furthermore, the one activity (steering) and its narrative space (the boat) is defined implicitly by the other more dominant narrative space, the jungle and the barbarous activities it seems to invite. This whole dimension is nowhere represented in Conrad's professional log.

But to repeat, the exercise is not to assign Conrad points for 'accuracy'; rather it is a question of discerning how narratives embody and determine a way of looking by highlighting some facets of a possible realization and 'underlighting' others.

We have now established some of the general features of Marlow's narrative:

1 social isolation,
2 description of and contemplation on the wilderness as mystery,
3 the re-surfacing of work as a theme (but this time as a personal physical activity rather than as a generalized feature of social and economic life), and
4 the displacement of Kurtz's arrival in the narrative.

(ii) The Uses of Isolation

But how do these elements interrelate? To answer this let us look closely at Marlow's description of the up-river journey. Remembering that describing is always *inscribing* (of meanings, ways of looking), let's consider how Marlow's account prefigures and frames his understanding of Kurtz and the meaning of Kurtz's experience. **Why does his 'description' place such emphasis on social isolation? And how does the way he contemplates the land affect his thinking about himself and Kurtz? Finally, why the deferring of the arrival, in the narrative, of Kurtz?**

DISCUSSION

The accentuated sense of oppressive isolation seems first of all to highlight Marlow's narrative role as a lone venturer in search of an even more isolated 'explorer'. Edwardian readers would hardly have ignored shades of Stanley's much publicized search for Dr Livingstone, even if Conrad's dismissive reference to 'newspaper stunts'[5] seeks to deny the connection. And in itself it explores a powerful narrative myth, while Kurtz's dilapidated outpost, surrounded and made inaccessible by wilderness, confirms the narrative model. At the same time, the emphasis on isolation 'elevates' the solitariness and thus the symbolic eminence of Kurtz as an 'enchanted princess' sleeping in a fabulous tower (p. 77), even if the gender attribution is intriguing!

Social isolation also transforms the wilderness from a site of economic colonization to that goal of individual heroic endeavour, where the isolated figure is seen, not as a 'trader' or 'colonizer,' but rather as an 'adventurer' loosed from the geographical and cultural constraints of 'civilized' Europe and having to discover 'his own true stuff' in confrontation with the inscrutable 'other' – the mysterious, impenetrable jungle. To repeat, it is not that Marlow actually *is* alone; the head-count undercuts that supposition. But in the form and direction that Marlow's narrative takes with the up-river journey, it seems to me that Marlow thinks of himself, and represents himself, as separate. The (politically critical) observer is transformed into the lone venturer and contemplative witness.

There are other historical-ideological features of the writing which amplify this impression. Read again carefully pages 66–70, from 'Going up that river . . .' to 'There was surface truth enough in these things to save a wiser man'. **What specific references, or we may say traces, of time – and passing time – do you notice? What tense, for example, does Marlow use to recount the action? Look also at the depiction of the wilderness and how it is peopled. What qualities and meanings does Marlow attribute to them? How does he respond to these qualities? Finally, look at the way Marlow perceives himself in relation to others.**

DISCUSSION

The most striking thing for me concerning time is the constant emphasis on the journey towards Kurtz as a journey that goes back in time to some primeval past, 'in the night of the first ages'. What is primordial and has been long forgotten suddenly becomes present again. The prehistoric is the here and now.

At the stylistic level I noticed in the tense chosen a kind of formal repetition, too, which underlines the idea of return and retardation. It is a way of narrating which suggests time suspended, an always having done something. More or less identical occurrences are described once in the iterative past tense, which suggests an almost habitual frequency of events. The numerous actions thus rendered – 'I watched for sunken stones', 'you lost your way', 'as we struggled round the bend there would be a glimpse of rush walls' – are conveyed in a tense which perfectly mirrors a sense of time suspended. Marlow says that the journey took some two months. But the rhythms of repetition and recurrence (on a formal and on a proairetic level – i.e. the level of actions) not surprisingly confirm what he repeats is the overwhelming impact of the journey. It seemed like a trip of immense return, a trip into prehistory. 'Going up that river was like travelling back to the earliest beginnings of the world. . . . We were wanderers on prehistoric earth.'

On the face of it, this sense of retardation and return, the implications of this temporality, strike me as rather paradoxical. Ostensibly we are moving forward in the narrative towards Kurtz. He himself, we may recall, has been described by the brickmaker as one of the new (advance) guard. But if it is an advance, it is one via returns and beginnings. With the repetition of actions, and with the reiterated sense of the prehistoric, time – far from being a linear movement forward – is held in suspension or returns on itself.

The narrative delay in getting to Kurtz is starting to look like something more than a device to create audience excitement through suspension. The narrative drive for the reader, like Marlow's compunction, may be to answer the enigma, 'Who is Kurtz? What is he really like? What does he signify?' But this drive seems to be retarded both on the 'content' level of the narrative (we go back to prehistory) and the formal level (the iterative tense). How does this come to structure the way Kurtz is (finally) perceived and understood? How might this particular figuring of time work? Is it only an incidental narrative feature or might it have ideological implications implying a specific, though on Marlow's part a possibly unacknowledged, way of looking and of construing Kurtz?

But at this point you may have an objection. **What is all the fuss about? Aren't these passages just rather lush descriptive interludes filling the narrative space until Marlow gets to Kurtz, or at least until the action picks up with the attack on the boat? Don't we mentally label them bits of exotic travelogue, the sort of filler passages we needn't attend to too closely?**

DISCUSSION

Think of the assumptions underlying these objections. They suggest that narrative space preexists Marlow's telling of the tale and that he has to fill the gap. But there will only be a gap if the narrator chooses to make one. He could have hastened the narration of his meeting with Kurtz by eliding these long descriptive passages and cutting, for example, his own admittedly digressive browsing through Towson's manual of seamanship, or the nine-page interview with its owner, the Russian. (Compared to the twelve or so pages devoted to Marlow's actual encounter with Kurtz in person, this, by the way, seems surprisingly disproportionate and increases the sense of delay and suspension.) So why the delay? **Why does Marlow spend so much narrative time getting to what seems to be the goal of the story – the figure of Kurtz and the answer to the question (in all its possible implications), 'Who is Kurtz?'**

DISCUSSION

One possible answer to Marlow's 'delay' is that any narrative based on the hermeneutic structure of question and answer – and in this regard *Heart of Darkness* can be thought of as corresponding to the hermeneutic type of the detective story – will of necessity be driven by two countervailing needs and forces.[6] The drive to closure (realization, answer, truth) will be in tension with the constraining force to withhold closure and maintain the enigma. Reading would involve the desire to entertain both contradictory drives at once. Each requires the other. Put simply, we enjoy the suspense. Can we attribute to Marlow this sort of consideration for his listeners' appetite for the thrill of suspense? We might recall the framing narrator's remarks on Marlow's yarns (see p. 30 of the text) – that they were inconclusive, that perhaps they did not hold his audience in an unbearable state of anticipation. If suspense is at best only a partial function of the dilatory quality of narration, are there other possible reasons for the delay? Think of Shakespeare's *Hamlet*. On one level, Hamlet's situation contains the narrative and psychological imperative to take revenge on his father's murderer. The play relies on the pressure for that end to be held forever in view – but also for it to be delayed as long as possible. The drama depends for its existence not on the closing of the gap between injunction and execution, but on the interesting maintenance of its being kept open. If, as soon as he saw his father's ghost and heard his account, he felt no qualms or lack of opportunity but eliminated Claudius at once, we would have had a severely truncated and arguably weaker play. But would we say it is the suspense about Hamlet – what will he do? – which keeps us engaged with the play? My suspicion is that we would not. And by definition it couldn't be that suspense which keeps audiences and readers coming back to the play over and over. Indeed, I would argue that for any contemporary audience/reader, the narrative of Hamlet has already been 'read' in the sense that they have always already known what happens to Hamlet. If, then, with *Hamlet* suspension does not function primarily to create suspense, but rather to engage with profounder questions of Hamlet's self-understanding, so too with Marlow's tale we might more fruitfully ask, 'With what does Marlow fill the narrative gap and delay he's created? And what does it mean?' Consider particularly pp. 66–70.

(iii) The Meanings of Meaninglessness

Talking specifically of such passages as these, the critic F. R. Leavis actually thought they meant very little. And he used the phrase 'adjectival insistence' to dismiss them, as I've already indicated in Chapter 4. For him they are repetitive and evasive – marking Conrad's inability to rise above the meaningless. He acknowledges Conrad's achievement in engendering 'the overwhelming sinister and fantastic "atmosphere"' by means of an 'art of vivid essential record in terms of things seen and incidents experienced by a main agent in the narrative'. But he goes on to say:

> There are, however, places in *Heart of Darkness* where we become aware of comment as an interposition, and worse, as an intrusion, at

times an exasperating one. Hadn't he, we find ourselves asking, overworked 'inscrutable', 'inconceivable', 'unspeakable' and that kind of word already? – yet still they recur. Is anything added to the oppressive mysteriousness of the Congo by such sentences as: 'It was the stillness of an implacable force brooding over an inscrutable intention.'? The same vocabulary, the same adjectival insistence upon inexpressible and incomprehensible mystery, is applied to the evocation of human profundities and spiritual horrors: to magnifying a thrilled sense of the unspeakable potentialities of the human soul. The actual effect is not to magnify but rather to muffle.

and concludes,

Conrad must here stand convicted of borrowing the arts of the magazine writer (who has borrowed his, shall we say, from Kipling and Poe) in order to impose on his readers and on himself, for thrilled response, a 'significance' that is merely an emotional insistence on the presence of what he can't produce. The insistence betrays the absence, the willed 'intensity' the nullity. He is intent on making a virtue out of not knowing what he means.[7]

How satisfactory do you find this critique? Do you think Conrad should thus stand 'convicted' of not knowing what he means?

DISCUSSION

I agree with Leavis on the rendering of a sinister atmosphere and think the evidence of a 'vivid essential record' has been confirmed. I'm less happy with his slipping between Marlow and Conrad in referring to the narration. For all of Leavis's impressive emphasis on specific details, I noted that he fails to distinguish, even theoretically, between Conrad and his character. The creation of a 'thrilled response', for example, attributed to Conrad, must at least be seen as complicated by the fact that it is mediated by Marlow telling his story to a (more or less attentive, certainly fairly captive) audience. The fictional status of this telling and its particular audience can't be ignored. In other words, it is Marlow who says he cannot understand his experience – and so reiterates the inarticulable vague horror which annoys Leavis. But this seems altogether plausible: sometimes we do feel that something 'means', carries import, without being able to say quite what that is. Marlow's narrative mode seeks to render precisely that sense.

Leavis's account is also vulnerable to another objection if we put the question of meaning – or rather meaninglessness – another way around. (In doing so I think perhaps we are more critical even than Leavis.) Is it in fact true that Marlow simply produces in us a 'thrilled sense' of something heavy with meaninglessness? Something he

promises and fails to deliver? A 'nullity'? I would rather suggest that
on the contrary, this atmospheric evocation of the incomprehensible
becomes, paradoxically, its (meaningless) meaning and function.
What Marlow perceives as the 'inscrutability' of his surrounding is
the degree to which it threatens him. He is threatened because at any
time his thinking about it edges him towards the brink of realizing
three disturbing features about it. First, despite its otherness, he feels
a 'kinship' with it; second, he cannot comprehend and therefore
cannot control or contain it; and third, it, not he, is the source of
power and agency. What an ironic inversion of the valencies of
power between white man and colonized land – that this 'monster',
normally conquered and shackled (like the chain-gang), should be
'free' and so subject the isolated white to its powers! Note how,
incidentally, the master/slave structure of power which has characterized the colonizer/colonized relationship has not been abandoned
in Marlow's perceptions. Rather, the terms of the equation remain,
but with the references inverted.

This relationship of colonizer to colonized is one of dominant
possession. The colonizer assumes he owns and controls the colonized space and can use its indigenous inhabitants as he wishes.
Whereas previously Conrad, through Marlow, has been offering a
critique of the megalomaniac tendencies of this belief assumed in the
person of the colonizer, now the terms are reversed. The land is a
space not controlled by but controlling Marlow, just as it is later
shown to control Kurtz. He does not know it – but it looks
knowingly, inscrutably, purposively at him. Marlow sees in this
landscape a mirror image of the white man's act of possession.

**Thus, though calling it 'incomprehensible', Marlow proceeds to
attribute qualities to it, such as 'the prehistoric'. The meaningless
gathers meaning. Make a note of any of these qualities that strike
you.**

DISCUSSION

The landscape is 'implacable', pitiless – like, earlier, the 'rapacious
and pitiless folly' (p. 43) of the colonizers? It is also 'vengeful':
seeking to get its own back on these intruders?

With profound oxymoronic compulsion, Marlow elaborates on
the incomprehensible 'other': the earth is unearthly; it is monstrous
. . . and yet it is attractive and 'thrilling' to him. He feels like a 'sane
man before an enthusiastic outbreak in a madhouse'. So we can see
how this *describing* of the jungle as 'prehistoric' inscribes it with
potent meanings, however little Marlow is conscious of it. For as we
shall see, he is not keen to look too closely into the implications

evoked: 'I got used to it afterwards; I did not see it any more'. But to this sort of repression we will return shortly.

To *inscribe* this landscape as prehistoric evokes such a powerful European stereotype that we may take the myth as somehow self-evident, as natural, and allow other assumptions, too, to slip in, in its wake. **But learning from Marlow and critiquing his representations, let's first ask what ideological work this equation of the jungle as prehistoric is really doing. How does Marlow actually construe its inhabitants? What characteristics does he ascribe to them, inscribe them in?**

DISCUSSION

As I have already suggested, the natives are in no way individuated. They, too, are 'prehistoric'; their frenzied howling and dancing is, like the wilderness, monstrous and attractive, whose incomprehensibility and exotic 'otherness' is equally attributed to them. If the land is seen by Marlow as a site of return to prehistory, then its inhabitants, bodying forth this primal wildness, are barely differentiated from it. In their physical frenzy they are absorbed in their bodily parts into their surroundings. The landscape is thus virtually erased of 'the human' – in any social-cultural manifestation. Rejected, as it were, back into a distant past, the natives exist just this side of the inhuman. By another inversion, the wilderness is anthropomorphized – it has inscrutable purposes, the power to look; and later 'seemed to draw [Kurtz] to its pitiless breast' (p. 107). Moreover, human inhabitants, 'black hands, a mass of hands' (p. 68), are reduced, represented only as separate anatomical parts: 'I made out, deep in the tangled gloom, naked breasts, arms, legs, glaring eyes – the bush was swarming with human limbs in movement, glistening, of bronze colour' (p. 80).

This passage assimilates the human bodies into the trees and bushes, underscoring the stereotype of primitive savagery – the black as contemporary ancestor, as physical animal, as barely human body without intellect. Marlow's earlier perception of the black as colonized gives way to a different set of terms which draw upon, rather than deconstruct, European cultural stereotypes: the political theme of colonizer versus colonized is displaced by a different 'couple' – civilized vs. savage. How far its assumptions are endorsed, and how far they are questioned by Marlow, remains a question, but the theme of civilized/savage has been put on the agenda, and we will now need to turn to it.

(iv) Black Mistress, Black Cannibals

But before we do, is it fair to say that all the natives are henceforth portrayed as 'savages'? As you may object at this point, what about the figure of Kurtz's black mistress, or the black crew? Aren't they sufficiently specific? Don't they refute my accusation that Marlow, with sweeping generalization, invokes a dehumanized savage stereotype? Admittedly, there *are* critics who seem to think that to consider the black woman at all is excessive. As one such put it in referring to Conrad's depiction of women:

> *Heart of Darkness* . . . avoids what is Conrad's greatest fault, his inability to create convincing women characters, by keeping its only two women (Conrad's aunt and Kurtz's 'Intended') in the background.[8]

Spot the two obvious mistakes.

And then consider the depiction of Kurtz's mistress, the seventh woman the text makes reference to, along with the two knitters and the 'compassionate secretary' (of admittedly indeterminate sex) in the Company Office, Marlow's aunt, the accountant's native seamstress, and of course Kurtz's Intended.

Read carefully pages 100–1, from 'Dark human shapes . . .' to 'A formidable silence hung over the scene'. What do you think is connoted by the phrase 'wild and gorgeous apparition of a woman'? And why 'apparition'? Wouldn't just 'woman' do? Is she set off against, or seen to share the attributes of, the primitive savage which we've mentioned?

DISCUSSION

The phrase 'wild and gorgeous' seems to me to reinforce the oxymoronic definition, for Marlow, of the wilderness: utterly other and incomprehensible, it is nevertheless (or for that reason) fascinatingly attractive. True, the 'horrid faces', the 'monstrous' appearance of prehistoric man, have been replaced by a 'barbarous' beauty. But she stands, an incarnation of the seductiveness and potentially corrupting force of the savage wilderness, at one with and undifferentiated from it. She is its image, its soul. At the same time as her well-armoured appearance suggests the Amazonian stereotype, there is an emphasis in Marlow's depiction on the tragic dignity and sorrow which is somehow also present. Victim, like the wilderness, of the European invasion, she also threatens to be its vanquisher.

An intriguing word in this context is 'apparition', if we bear in mind her physical presence. It suggests, doesn't it, a questionable state of existence. Is she real? or imaginary? (The word 'figure' or 'appearance' would probably not have provoked quite the same degree of ambiguity.) 'Apparition' might cause us to question the status of the impression Marlow conveys of her. Echoing the sense of the 'unearthliness' of the earth, she is seen to occupy a space on the borderline between the real and the unreal, the human and the non-human, the material and the fantastic. And such a threshold is not an easy position to occupy. She mirrors the wilderness and bodies forth its sexual threat. I would suggest, in other words, that 'apparition' might alert us to the notion that for all her physicality she is an imaginative space (like the blank map?) onto which Marlow can inscribe the meanings of the European male gaze, while at the same time he can pass these meanings off as the inherent qualities of the object gazed at. And then 'discover' his kinship with it. As Oscar Wilde said of Wordsworth, 'He went to the lakes, but he was never a lake poet. He found in the stones the sermons he had already hidden there'.[9]

Perhaps in that sense it is, paradoxically, symptomatic after all that the innumerate critic quoted above does not see her or count her as an individuated woman, for any unique individuality has been rendered invisible. She functions as the sign of '(black) woman', though not, for once, in innocent quarantine, but rather (in mirror contradiction, for she's black) on the march. If O'Prey has written her off, Marlow has written her out, ex-pressed her: what we are seeing is not a black woman, a historically/culturally particular and realized individuality in difference, but rather the projections of the white European male mind. The inscrutable purpose and sexual threat of the wild is registered in the displaced phallic reaction of the Russian Harlequin:

> She turned away slowly, walked on, following the bank, and passed into the bushes to the left. Once only her eyes gleamed back at us in the dusk of the thickets before she disappeared.
> 'If she had offered to come aboard I really think I would have tried to shoot her', said the man of patches, nervously.   (p. 101)

How I, as a reader, have understood her is not without its implications, either. Did I call her Kurtz's mistress? Well, yes; as do other critics referring to her as his mistress or lover. **But this is something I infer from the text, isn't it? We are not directly told it. Where do I get the idea from? Did you make the same inferences?**

DISCUSSION

Neither Marlow talking to his listeners on board the *Nellie* nor Conrad and his implied reader (the reader assumed by the text) need (or perhaps even can) articulate the 'logic' of this inferred stereotype.

It is, however, as unspoken truth, available in the currency of literary and cultural discourse about Africa in late nineteenth- and twentieth-century European representations of the black native woman. The connotations are activated by a body of cultural 'knowledge' (that is, assumptions about difference) which confirm the black as 'passionate' and 'sexually active' and the black woman, specifically, as physical temptation or source of sexual gratification – for the reader as much as for the historical white traders, missionaries, etc., in 'darkest Africa'. The comparative nudity of African women was read as clear testimony of their abandoned sensuality. The power of this stereotype is its (for the audience/reader) self-evidence. Conrad may rise above his contemporaries in literary quality, but he by no means eschews all the terms of their discourse. The meanings this discourse inscribes reveal a lot about the colonizing mind, not its objects.

It is surely significant, too, that the black 'mistress' is kept at a distance. Neither narratively nor spatially does Marlow or the reader encounter her at close quarters. Although the Harlequin makes reference to her speaking, talking to Kurtz 'like a fury', she is not allowed to speak for herself in the narrative, only to be represented, spoken for, by Marlow and the Harlequin. We might want to attribute this to Marlow's predilection for the containment of women. Alternatively, as her relative silence is determined as much by Conrad's construction of the plot as by Marlow's mediation of his encounter, we might see Conrad as complicit with Marlow in this figuring of the woman. For nowhere in the narrative could I, at least, find anything which controverted the assumptions of Marlow's partial view of her. Though present in the narrative, she is a sort of absence, which Marlow can fill with his meanings. She does not need to speak because Marlow can see what she means, as it were. Of course, had she done so, had Marlow asked her about Kurtz or her cry, things might have been different. But that is another story.

This raises a central and critical question for the novel as a whole: when are partial or stereotypical forms of representation exposed to critique in the work and when are they quietly deployed and thus endorsed? Are there any theoretical 'rules of distribution' which condition either the deconstruction or deployment? The issue is fundamental because it bears upon so many aspects of the work: Conrad's critique of language and colonialism, arguments like Achebe's over his 'bloody racism', and the assessment of Kurtz's confrontation with the Wilderness are a few. In this respect the portrayal of the black crew provides a useful test-case, and I would argue counterpoint, to stereotypic representations of the 'savage'.

How does Marlow appraise the cannibal crewmen? We have

noticed in Chapter Four that Marlow acknowledges a sort of kinship with the fireman. Does the affiliation reach to other black crewmen? **Reread the depictions of the cannibals (pp. 67, 74–6) and note to what extent they confirm, or depart from, your expectations of them. Further, how do they compare to the savages on shore?**

DISCUSSION

Surely Marlow's almost throw-away reference to cannibalism ('Fine fellows – cannibals – in their place. They were men one could work with and I'm grateful to them') confounds, within the first phrase, the stereotypical representation of and stands in sharp contrast to those on shore. Marlow thus undermines the categories of frenzied passion and exotic culinary habits which, applied to those on shore, we are invited to entertain. A certain economy of distribution is implied – distance and proximity. Here, in the known space of the vessel, in immediate contact and negotiation with others, Marlow depicts blacks in wholly non-stereotypical ways which set them off against their 'counterparts' on shore. There, in that other space, absence of close engagement allows for a proliferation of generalized and mystifying categorization, and reproduces rather than critically examines the ideology inherent in its stereotypes.

Still, we have to ask: how far does the demystification of the cannibals go? What about the brief dialogue with their headman (p. 74)?

DISCUSSION

Well, yes, it is true that on one of the very few occasions in the novel when direct speech by blacks is actually recorded by Marlow, the white assumption of primitive cannibalism is almost jokingly asserted. But against that, I would suggest that the emphasis on their remarkable 'restraint' (a key word in Marlow's economy of civilized behaviour) outweighs it. This restraint is surprising even to Marlow, who acknowledges their immediate hunger and their superior number. Nor do they go ashore for a 'howl and a dance'. The strongest emphasis is placed not on any primitive tribal rites, but rather on them as 'relocated labour' and victims of economic exploitation. Their 'restraint' not only refutes their name; it also contradicts Marlow's understanding of what even 'civilized' man does when faced with starvation.[10]

> Yes; I looked at them as you would on any human being, with a curiosity of their impulses, motives, capacities, weaknesses, when brought to the test of an inexorable physical necessity. Restraint!

> What possible restraint? Was it superstition, disgust, patience, fear —
> or some kind of primitive honour? No fear can stand up to hunger, no
> patience can wear it out, disgust simply does not exist where hunger is;
> and as to superstition, beliefs, and what you may call principles, they
> are less than chaff in a breeze. (p. 76)

What literal cannibalism there might be, or is hinted at, is put at the
door of Kurtz (or just outside it). Metaphorical cannibalism — the
wilful consumption of human life — has already, of course, been well
documented by Marlow at the Outer Station, perpetrated by the
European emissaries of light.

However, this line of argument, and my sliding over of the
headman's (is that a Conradian joke?) speech, does point to inherent
contradictions in Marlow's position. It is as if he were trying to have
it both ways: he generally refutes the savage cannibal stereotype,
while simultaneously being willing to exploit it, if only momentarily,
in melodramatic speech, as a sop to an audience for whom the
cannibal was a well-established figure of fear and thus joke, in later
nineteenth-century representations of Africa. Just as with the black
woman, here also we may have a case of complicity on Conrad's
part, which reinforces his white readership's complacency for one
moment while in his depiction of the blacks' restraint he is also and
predominantly assaulting it.

In summary, I would suggest that in his varied depictions of 'savages'
Marlow is a long way from adopting a coherent point of view:
'restrained' cannibals on the boat are nevertheless said to feel rather
peckish for those on shore. They work hard and command greater
respect than Marlow's panicky pilgrims, who show little restraint at
all under pressure. The barely human howling frenzy of the 'prehistoric savages' on shore is pagan and mysterious, yet evokes in
Marlow an enthralling sense of kinship. The sexual, barbarous
woman is also magnificent and stately. The fireman is foolishly,
superstitiously prey to white 'witchcraft', yet shares Marlow's concentration on the immediate task in hand.

So as the colonialist vs. colonized theme gives way to a new
configuration — the 'civilized' vs. the 'savage' — a different kind of
historical trace emerges for our attention: not history as content
(depicted events) but rather the history of a system of representations
which Marlow employs in the depiction, a specific history of ways of
looking. For as with all texts, there is the issue of 'intertextuality':
Conrad's novel draws heavily upon a body of cultural texts rich in
images and assumptions about Africa and the African as primitive
which pervaded mid and late nineteenth-century European culture —
and which still have their powerful representatives today. (A recent

political cartoon, for example, portrayed a Liberal Party–SDP power struggle in terms of grass-skirted black cannibals heating a cauldron ready for the reception of one of their opposite numbers.) By 'cultural texts' I mean not just adventure novels, but manifold other literary forms – travel journals, missionary reports, newspapers, illustrated magazines – and mass cultural enterprises like the Great Exhibition of 1851 or subsequent World Fairs or Scientific Exhibitions. Via such media, Africa and the African were being represented for European understanding and 'consumption' in ways which produced and endorsed stereotypic images of this 'other'. This process, in turn, came to condition subsequent experiences and perceptions of Africa. When they went and conquered, they saw what they'd been *prepared* to see. The 'savage' and the darkest wild, even when seen 'for the first time', were always already known.[11]

(v) Conrad and Darwinism

One of the most powerful sources of influence in the production of these representations, and one that underpins Conrad's own work, was the developing 'science' of anthropology, and specifically the theories of Darwin, which generated a discourse on the 'primitive' soon to be absorbed and circulated among the general populace.

Darwin's *The Origin of Species* appeared in 1859. His evolutionary theory of species was subsequently developed, particularly in the work of Herbert Spencer, and adapted as a social theory of racial development. This latter form of 'Social Darwinism' came to dominate late nineteenth-century scientific, specifically anthropological, thinking and had a wider and profoundly influential currency within the popular imagination. It offered a framework and discourse by which white Europeans came to understand their related origins to, but differential development from, other races.

According to this schema, man has not (as the Bible proposes) been created specially and separately from other animals – nor has woman, either. Rather, humankind has descended and evolved from them over aeons of time, in struggle with and adaptation to the environment. Thus an inherent animal nature is accorded to the human, at least in its primal form. Almost co-eval with this evolution, however, is the (alleged) development of racial differences, located by Darwin and his successors so far back in prehistory as to make those differences 'primordial'. In this scenario, social and cultural developments of different races are themselves differential – Europeans have adapted and evolved to a higher level befitting the survival of the 'fittest'; Africans peculiarly have not evolved since reaching a (for them) ultimate level of evolution in the distant past.

Africa can then come to be seen as representing a 'living museum' of earlier levels of human progress. A powerful conjunction which metaphorically embraces the anthropological with the proto-Freudian can then be identified in the perception of 'primitive', 'savage' Africans as the 'children' of the civilized. As Spencer puts it: 'the intellectual traits of the uncivilized are . . . traits recurring in the children of the civilized'.[12]

The mixture of 'scientific' and ideological interests should be apparent in this model. Darwin's own writings occasionally let the 'scientific' mask fall to reveal attitudes which lend credence to and feed the imagery of stereotypes I've spoken of:

> The main conclusion arrived at in this work, namely that man is descended from some lowly organised form, will, I regret to think, be highly distasteful to many. But there can hardly be a doubt that we are descended from barbarians. The astonishment which I felt on first seeing a party of Fuegians on a wild and broken shore will never be forgotten by me, for the reflection at once rushed into my mind – such were our ancestors. These men were absolutely naked and bedaubed with paint, their long hair was tangled, their mouths frothed with excitement, and their expression was wild, startled, and distrustful. They possessed hardly any arts, and like wild animals lived on what they could catch; they had no government, and were merciless to every one not of their own small tribe. He who has seen a savage in his native land will not feel much shame, if forced to acknowledge that the blood of some more humble creature flows in his veins. For my own part I would as soon be descended from that heroic little monkey, who braved his dreaded enemy in order to save the life of his keeper, or from that old baboon, who descending from the mountains, carried away in triumph his young comrade from a crowd of astonished dogs – as from a savage who delights to torture his enemies, offers up bloody sacrifices, practises infanticide without remorse, treats his wives like slaves, knows no decency, and is haunted by the grossest superstitions.[13]

This brief canter into the historical context of cultural representations can help us to locate more precisely Conrad's complex relationship to it. **Compare this with Conrad's portrait of the savage. What things does Conrad endorse, and how far does he distance himself from the thinking represented in Darwin's account?**

DISCUSSION

You may think it unfair to draw the comparison. After all, Darwin is talking about Terra del Fuegians and Conrad's work is not (though, as we have mentioned at the start, he does not explicitly name Africa). But that is as much the point as an objection to the comparison. For primarily Darwin is talking about the 'barbarian', and I think for nineteenth-century readers there would have been no trouble in transferring the one location to another via the common terms, 'savage' and 'barbarian'. Wherever s/he may be, the 'barbarian' is the 'other' to the civilized European. Geography and history can be elided by the lowest common multiple, 'savage'.

In Conrad, the image of 'savage' as ancestor is endorsed; but not the concomitant 'disgust'. On the contrary, Marlow feels enthralled by the kinship. This is surely the crux and Conrad's real project in engaging with the 'civilized' vs. the 'savage' opposition. For his strategy is to propose the contrast but redistribute the defining terms of it. Qualities which are attributed to the 'savage' are shared by the 'civilized'. He thus critically undermines the 'progressive' thrust of the Darwinian view of evolutionary social development by suggesting that the 'civilized' is nothing more than the 'primitive' dressed up in 'pretty rags – rags that would fly off at the first good shake' (p. 69). Looking at the savage, then, we can see there not, with superior complacency, the image of our ancestors, but rather the truth of ourselves, stripped of the 'cloak' (to reiterate Marlow's metaphor) of time. Thus weird incantations and drum beats are not contrasted but compared with Christian church bells, and it is 'forgotten and brutal instincts' which drive 'civilized' Kurtz into the wilderness. In sum, the binary opposition civilized/savage is radically questioned by the text.

Yet at the same time, it is not. Consider again my formulation: 'qualities of the "savage" are shared by the "civilized"'? The civilized is 'nothing more than' the barbarian? My language accepts the system of representation – postulates the existence and attributes of 'primitive savage' even as it critiques 'civilization'. Marlow's language (reinforced by Conrad's narrative structure – a return to beginnings) does the same. The idea of the savage is inscribed in the text in order to be subsequently revealed (in Marlow's responses and the experience of Kurtz) as the dark underside of civilized Europe. It exists as a white male construction of the 'other' to mirror and articulate the European. In short, if the black savage doesn't actually exist, it has to be invented by the European to define not the alien 'darkness' but the European self. Whether radical or complacent, the concept 'European' entails and needs the concept 'savage', which paradoxically reaffirms ethnocentricity. On the complacent, Darwinian 'progressive' view, the European is defined via negation – the European civilized is what the savage is not (and vice versa). On the Conradian view, definition is via analogy: we, too, are savage. But note the cultural egoism of both views, an egoism reflected in another critic, even closer to home. To cite again my own formulation:

The European colonial encounter with Africa and Africans gives way to civilized man's deeper encounter with himself.[14]

'Civilized'? 'Deeper'? Isn't there a kind of cultural arrogance in such ideas, hardly less imperialistic in its imaginative drive than with the politically more explicit colonial issue? For don't both say, 'What's really important is me'?[15]

No wonder this 'necessary' construction of the savage produces contradictions – particularly when it comes slap bang up against a reality which confutes it. We've already noted that 'savage' attributes aren't arbitrarily designated to all blacks, though. When Marlow feels he is in close and personal engagement with 'savages', he is able, in effect, to unpack the very stereotypic representations he accepts when his perspective on them is more distanced, generalized, and 'contemplative'. To generalize from this (the contradiction is not ignored), for Conrad, an 'objective', distanced view does not, as a rationalist culture proposes, guarantee truth; rather, it might replicate a form of blindness.

To summarize, this chapter has highlighted a new and central thematic issue in the novel: 'civilization and savagery'. This emerges with a shift in narrative focus from the political and historical thrust of early sections of the work – the critique of colonialism – to the ostensibly more 'philosophical' concern of civilized European man confronting the wilderness.

I stressed how the formal features of the narrative – how Conrad has Marlow tell his story – are employed in this shift. The emphasis on social isolation, the radical treatment of time, Marlow's 'adjectival insistence' on mystery, for instance – all contribute to the philosophical questioning of the relationship of 'civilized' to savage.

Conrad's radical insight into this relationship lies in Marlow's recognition of the closeness of the two. However mysterious and inscrutable, savagery is not something so utterly alien that it has no connection with European man. On the contrary, the wilderness mirrors what is present and lurking beneath the skin of civilized people were they but to know and acknowledge it.

But – and it is a big 'but' – I argue that this insight, Marlow's description of the savage as horrible and desirable, alien and close, is itself a political reading or construction of the African. The novel relies heavily and unconsciously on the European, essentially male, cultural stereotypes of the 'savage', however much it might and does profoundly question some aspects of them. For that reason we should really read the words 'civilized' and 'savage' with heavy inverted commas, for we are always dealing with ethnocentric cultural representations of the other which are, after all, unconsciously, historical and political.

My emphasis on Marlow as a reader, supplying as much as

descrying meanings, is a consistent thread running through the following chapter, too. In it, I will discuss four key issues: first, Marlow's portrayal of Kurtz, particularly the functions of Kurtz's voice; second, the possible meanings of Kurtz's cry; third, Marlow's lie to the Intended – which reintroduces the topic of the representation of the female in the novel; and finally, the issue of Marlow's storytelling itself.

In discussing these subjects, I will of necessity be inviting you to think about their bearing on the novel as a whole and will, correspondingly, rely less heavily on close tutorial discussion of specific passages.

6. Endings: Crying, Dying, Lying . . . and Telling Stories

Every sentence is a sentence of death.   *Oscar Wilde*

'I see what you mean', says Marlow. 'Speak for yourself', says the wilderness and the 'savage'. That, I have been suggesting, is what Marlow claims and what the 'savage', if allowed to speak rather than be spoken for, might have answered back. At any rate, Marlow's claim provides him with a frame of perception through which Kurtz is anticipated and through which Marlow figures him as revealing the humanly primal; he embodies elemental truth 'stripped of its cloak of time' (p. 69) and stripped, too, of the illusory protective veneer of 'civilization' and social niceties. For Marlow's narrative insists that Kurtz has been there; Kurtz has seen it all. What 'it' is – and whether and how it can ever be told – is the concern of this chapter.

(i) Endings

Endings are perhaps the hardest things to achieve in fiction. 'For to end, yet again', as Beckett puts it. Like the 'false beginnings' to *Heart of Darkness*, there are several endings, with which the novel seems successively to culminate.

Any one of the following might be a candidate: Marlow's midnight struggle with Kurtz; Kurtz's cry and death; Marlow's lie to the Intended; or the final full-stop! Let us consider them in turn.

Marlow's midnight chase after Kurtz is one culminating point (pp. 106–8), pushing Marlow to the very extremities of his relation with Kurtz. 'If anybody had ever struggled with a soul, I am the man. . . . I saw it – I heard it. I saw the inconceivable mystery of a soul that knew no restraint, no faith, and no fear, yet struggling blindly with itself' (p. 108). After a claim like this, what could follow but a quiet coda?

Or there's Kurtz's death-bed cry, 'The horror! The horror!' We do not need to know that T. S. Eliot originally chose these words as the epigraph to *The Waste Land* to sense in them the authority of narrative and rhetorical summation – Kurtz speaking not just for himself but somehow for all humanity.

Kurtz dies (how could we imagine anything else, after his cry?) but Marlow survives to return to the living/dead in the 'sepulchral city' and a recapitulation of Kurtz's story to the latter's fiancée. And this moment, occurring one year later, is not climactic merely because of the drama of Marlow's telling (or not telling) Kurtz's last words. For Marlow, that earlier 'ending' seems to overlay and be co-present with the later one. The pressure of the first is not dispersed but rather accumulated in the second:

> while I waited [at the Intended's door] he seemed to stare at me out of the glassy panel. . . . I seemed to hear the whispered cry, 'The horror! The horror!' . . . the impression was so powerful that for me, too, he seemed to have died only yesterday – nay, this very minute, I saw her and him in the same instant of time – his death and her sorrow. . . . Do you understand? I saw them together.   (pp. 117–18)

Marlow's lie to the Intended does not just round off Kurtz's story; it finishes it off, bluntly contradicting everything Marlow has come to learn and thereby putting an end, with 'a taint of death' (p. 57), to any claim Marlow may make to veracity or authority. What *could* come after that? Well, the last paragraph, and an almost cyclical return to the opening situation of Marlow's story-telling aboard the *Nellie* on the Thames.

Four sorts of endings: crying, dying, lying and story-telling. I said one seemed 'embedded' in the next, but not in a mechanical way, like a structure of chinese boxes. Rather, one climactic moment somehow *generates the need* for the next – indeed, in a broad sense, generates the need to tell another story. The 'endings' almost relate like a genealogy: 'And the midnight chase begat Kurtz's cry. And Kurtz's cry begat Marlow's lie. And Marlow's lie begat Marlow's tale'. In this authorized version, one narrative both gives authority to and motivates as author the next narrator.

To pin this down, let me invite you to consider each such moment as a narrative situation, or, more specifically, as a situation of some form of truth-telling. Each involves a claim to an experience, the possession of special knowledge, which could be passed on to a receiving audience. The audience does not necessarily want to hear what it gets; but it does want *something* to be passed on. So, a voice, an experience, and the telling of that experience to a listener: that is what all have in common.

Let us look first at Marlow's encounter with Kurtz and his death-cry: as a truth-telling situation it promises a lot. As I mentioned in connection with the hermeneutic structure of enigma – that search for a (possibly secret) answer to a question or problem (see p. 71) – we anticipate their meeting as the primal moment of the work (in all senses of 'primal'). Its narrative position suggests it is going to explain Marlow's journey. For even in retrospect, on the *Nellie*, he calls it 'the culminating point of [his] experience'. Furthermore, apart from what may be the truth-content of Kurtz's utterance – whatever 'The horror! The horror!' actually 'means' – the fact of its *occurrence* powerfully fulfils the long-deferred satisfaction of Marlow's desire to hear Kurtz's voice.

Has Marlow consistently had this idea of Kurtz as an impressive 'voice'? Think back over the information others have imparted to him about Kurtz. You might look particularly at the various accounts offered at the Outer Station by the Accountant (pp. 46–7) and at the Central Station, by the Manager and the Brickmaker (pp. 51–8) as well as that between the Manager and his uncle which Marlow inadvertently overhears (pp. 63–6). Has Marlow been intrigued from the outset? Does his attitude shift? What 'qualities' in Kurtz impress him?

DISCUSSION

I noted quite a shift in Marlow's attitude by no means commensurate with others' accounts. First there is a mild inquiry (p. 47) which is easily outweighed by the enthusiasm of the Accountant for this 'remarkable person'. Then he shows weary irritation at the Manager's praise for his 'best agent', 'an exceptional man, of the greatest importance to the Company'. 'Hang Kurtz, I thought' (p. 51) is Marlow's succinct response. The Brickmaker, arouses amused disbelief with his talk of this 'universal genius' (p. 58). In short, for a long time Marlow 'wasn't very interested in him' (p. 62).

So as an unwilling audience to this series of stories about Kurtz, Marlow shows slight interest. Insofar as Kurtz is portrayed as a 'better' type of Company agent, Marlow's disillusion with *that* whole enterprise relegates Kurtz to the worst of a bad lot. So where does the turning-point come?

It would seem to me to be when Marlow *overhears* a fragmentary account of Kurtz, when he is the unwitting and unacknowledged audience to the manager's disjointed conversation with his uncle. It is as if the tale *not told*, or rather the tale suggested but never explicit, is much more powerful in its effects on Marlow than the tales of remarkable performance enthusiastically thrust upon him. Now for the first time, Marlow says, he feels he can *see* Kurtz. He pictures him not as an outstanding company man, but, on the contrary, refusing this role – turning back up-river, back into the wilderness and away from the Central Station and the 'civilization' he had meant to rejoin. Perhaps in this imagined gesture lies one of the motivations for Marlow's subsequent 'choice of nightmares'.

Out of snatches of conversation overheard Marlow forms a picture, and it gives Marlow the first real motivation for his journey up-river:

> I was then rather excited at the prospect of meeting Kurtz very soon. . . . Where the pilgrims imagined [the steamboat] crawled to I don't know. . . . For me it crawled towards Kurtz – exclusively.   (pp. 66, 68)

Strong words of positive self-commitment and enthusiasm, coming from the hitherto sardonic Marlow!

But what do you make of his *interpretation* of his image of Kurtz turning back up-river?

> I did not know the motive [for Kurtz's return]. Perhaps he was just simply a fine fellow who stuck to his work for its own sake. His name, you understand, had not been pronounced once. He was 'that man'.   (p. 64)

Marlow, himself now the 'audience', has completed the story he has overheard, filling up the gaps (of motivation, of reference, even) by projecting on to it his own, self-confirmatory reading. After all, it is *Marlow's* ethic of work-for-its-own-sake which is being evinced here. And he may be hearing in the manager's contemptuous 'that man' a reference to a potential ally against the Company. In other words, Marlow seems to be creating his own story about Kurtz *against* those offered to him. The *reader* in Marlow is once again determining what he 'sees'.

(ii) The Voice

Once thus motivated by the imagined *seeing* of Kurtz, Marlow's interest is displaced by an imagined *hearing* of him. He is surprised to recognize this in the aftermath of the native attack on the steamboat, when he is forced to conclude that Kurtz must already be dead.

Look at the following passage and note the implicit terms of contrast Marlow is setting up.

'He is dead', murmured the fellow, immensely impressed. 'No doubt about it', said I, tugging like mad at the shoe-laces. 'And by the way, I suppose Mr Kurtz is dead as well by this time.'

For the moment that was the dominant thought. There was a sense of extreme disappointment, as though I had found out I had been striving after something altogether without a substance. I couldn't have been more disgusted if I had travelled all this way for the sole purpose of talking with Mr Kurtz. Talking with . . . I flung one shoe overboard and became aware that that was exactly what I had been looking forward to – a talk with Kurtz. I made the strange discovery that I had never imagined him doing, you know, but as discoursing. I didn't say to myself 'Now I will never see him' or 'Now I will never shake him by the hand' but, 'Now I will never hear him'. The man presented himself as a voice. Not, of course, that I did not connect him with some sort of action. Hadn't I been told in all the tones of jealousy and admiration that he had collected, bartered, swindled or stolen more ivory than all the other agents together? That was not the point. The point was in his being a gifted creature and that of all his gifts the one that stood out pre-eminently, that carried with it a sense of real presence, was his ability to talk, his words – the gift of expression, the bewildering, the illuminating, the most exalted and the most contemptible, the pulsating stream of light, or the deceitful flow from the heart of an impenetrable darkness. (pp. 82–3)

DISCUSSION

I think the clearest antithesis is that between doing (action) and talking. And it's worth remarking here that for Marlow 'talking' is not spoken of as some sort of action. It is *talking* which Marlow recognizes as Kurtz's greatest 'gift'. I noted other oppositions too – absence (or emptiness) and presence, for example. Kurtz is a man 'without a substance' but his voice somehow guarantees him 'a real presence', nevertheless. 'The man *presented* himself to me as a voice' (my italics).

Just think of the paradoxes implicit in this! A *voice* – which, remember, Marlow has not yet heard – seems more substantial, more tangible than actions: all those remarkable deeds which Marlow has, so to speak, heard talk of. And yet how ephemeral speech, unheard speech, must seem, particularly in the days before mechanical recording. Furthermore, 'voice' does seem in some ways to straddle the apparent dichotomy between absence and presence. 'I can hear his voice now' can sometimes mean 'I can hear something here and now, which *is not* here' – the always present voice of a dead friend, for example. 'Voice' can take on connotations evoked by 'ghost', 'presences' and 'haunting'. Indeed immediately after the present passage it is this *haunting* which preoccupies Marlow:

> A voice. He was very little more than a voice. And I heard – him – it – this voice – other voices – all of them were so little more than voices – and the memory of that time itself lingers around me, impalpable, like a dying vibration of one immense jabber, silly, atrocious, sordid, savage or simply mean, without any kind of sense. (p. 84)

Kurtz's voice is portrayed as contradictory. It is both 'illuminating' (light-bringing, truth-revealing) *and* deceitful, bewildering. It is an eloquence both exalted *and* contemptible. In earlier chapters we considered in detail the theme of discourse in the political context of colonial power. (See, for example, pp. 45–6) I suggested there that rhetoric, the persuasive use of language, was as important a component of exploitative control as physical or military force and that Marlow's immediate experience revealed that fact to him. Now, Marlow emphasizes Kurtz's voice as his primary gift, but still foregrounds its deeply ambivalent qualities. Eloquence is a double-headed creature, which holds no automatic guarantee of truth-telling or moral insight.

In this there is an echo of Conrad's sceptically equivocal attitude to eloquent speech or writing. In a preface to a cookery book his wife Jessie wrote, Conrad comments: 'Of all the books produced since the most remote ages by human talents and industry those only that treat of cooking are, from a moral point of view, above suspicion. The intention of every other piece of prose may be discussed and even mistrusted. . .'.[1] For with recipes – and if pushed Conrad probably would have added seamanship manuals like Towson's – language seems to stand in an immediate one-to-one functional relationship with its referent in the practical world. Its discourse is unambiguous and its purpose and interest clear and benign. How different Kurtz's words are, in speech or writing!

Look at the passage describing Marlow's reading of Kurtz's 'beautiful piece of writing', the report to the International Society for

the Suppression of Savage Customs (pp. 86–7). Here is what Ian Watt says about Marlow's reaction. Do you agree with him?

> Kurtz's rhetoric has no meaning for Marlow: for him it is merely 'one immense jabber' because it has no reference either to the real Kurtz or to the world Marlow has experienced.[2]

DISCUSSION

I think Watt wants to see only one side of the coin. Marlow recognizes *both* its mendacity *and* its effectiveness. He sees the gaps and contradictions between signified and signifier, between what he actually knows to be the case, and the way Kurtz represents it, gaps and contradictions which persuasive verbal structures can so easily conceal. But – and this is crucial – Marlow acknowledges that the eloquence can charm and arouse even him to near-adoration:

> From that point he soared and took me with him. The peroration was magnificent. . . . It made me tingle with enthusiasm. (p. 87)

Marlow nevertheless counters this euphoria with the comment that he was 'not prepared to affirm [Kurtz] was exactly worth the life we lost in getting him. I missed my late helmsman awfully'. Marlow thus oscillates between extremes in assessing Kurtz.

But note, Marlow doesn't fully confront this contradiction in his own response. Despite his 'enthusiasm' for Kurtz's words, consider what happens when Marlow encounters someone else who is similarly enthusiastic. **Look at his exchanges with the Russian Harlequin (especially pp. 94–5, 97–8). What is Marlow's reaction to the latter's talk of Kurtz? As you consider this, bear in mind the chronological order of his meeting the Russian and his reading the report and the order in which they are narrated by Marlow. Why do you think Conrad would organize the narrative sequence in this way?**

DISCUSSION

On the face of it Marlow is scathing in his dismissal of the Russian's naïve sycophancy, which can be moved by eloquence yet be blind to atrocity. Marlow understandably distances himself, adopting the higher and firmer moral ground:

> The tone of these words [about Kurtz's talk] was so extraordinary that I looked at him searchingly. It was curious to see his mingled eagerness and reluctance to speak of Kurtz . . . I suppose it did not occur to him that Mr Kurtz was no idol of mine. He forgot I hadn't heard any of these splendid monologues on, what was it? on love, justice, conduct of life or what not. (pp. 95, 98)

Accepting Marlow's own assessment (as Watt, above, essentially does), we could leave it at that. Strictly speaking, judged in terms of *story-time* – the chronology of events – Marlow is right. He has not heard any 'splendid monologues' – not yet. That itself begs the important question, to which we will return, as to why then Marlow *has* so forcefully imagined Kurtz as a voice.

But in terms of the narrative order – the order we experience in our reading – Marlow has already talked of reading Kurtz's report. Conrad has reversed the order of events to present Kurtz's report first (p. 86). Marlow's discussion of it is proleptic, anticipating a reading of the pamphlet given to Marlow some time later, certainly after he has talked to the Russian.

This narrative juxtaposition cannot be ignored. Conrad's narrative method denies itself an external authorial voice to pass commentary and final judgement on Marlow. But the narrative structure itself – i.e. the juxtaposition – frees the reader into a new perspective on Marlow. It proposes comparison and invites us to consider parallels and similarities between Marlow and the Russian, not just recognize their obvious differences. The narrative can reveal, without comment, how Marlow's angry response to the Russian conceals real inconsistencies: for *both* enthuse over Kurtz's eloquence. And the similarities go further.

While both 'soar' on Kurtz's rhetoric, they both have a deep respect and affection for that other more down-to-earth prose which stands at the opposite end of the rhetorical spectrum: Towson's seamanship manual. Marlow has described this as 'something unmistakably real [offering . . .] the shelter of an old and solid friendship' (pp. 71–2). The Russian's patch-work clothing is for Marlow a piece of beautiful workmanship and might metonymically remind us of Marlow's own labours at patching up his steamer. Both men are regarded by the Company as outsiders, friends of Kurtz, interlopers of sorts on the scene of managed exploitation. Clearly, Marlow is disdainful about the Russian's hero-worship of Kurtz and his readiness to ignore his excesses, calling him in his unmeditated devotion 'Kurtz's last disciple'. But Marlow, who has already admitted, 'I can't choose. He won't be forgotten. Whatever he was, he was not common', subsequently acknowledges an undying loyalty of sorts:

> I did not betray Mr Kurtz – it was ordered I should never betray him – it was written I should be loyal to the nightmare of my choice. (p. 105)

And that which he finds so curiously frightful when the Russian starts describing it – 'the ceremonies used when approaching Kurtz' (p. 97), details of which 'would be more intolerable than those heads drying on stakes' – is precisely what Marlow enacts later when he finds Kurtz in the forest:

> And don't you see, the terror of the position . . . was . . . that I had to deal with a being to whom I could not appeal in the name of anything high or low. I had, even like the niggers, to invoke him – himself – his own exalted and incredible degradation. (p. 107)

This last phrase, like the recognition of the loyalty to a *nightmare*, does imply a serious qualification of whole-hearted obedience. I am not suggesting a case of doubles here – although the Russian does literally step into Marlow's shoes! However, these uncanny and ironic parallels cast Marlow's narrative and judgemental 'reliability' in a new light. They reveal Marlow, yet again, as a partial and interested *reader* of others. His brusque and repelled reaction to the Russian, on one level explicable as moral contempt, might on another stem from his half-perceiving in the other man a dim reflection of himself. He projects on to the Russian not the traits themselves – they are all too real – but a shocked disdain for what he fears to trace in himself.

(iii) The Function of Kurtz

Contradiction and inconsistency also typify Marlow's portrayal of Kurtz. He is not merely 'ambiguous' and 'complex' – favoured terms for mature characterization in novels of psychological realism. In Marlow's narrative (that is, in Marlow's reading of him) he functions in ways which refuse an unequivocal and coherent reading. To illustrate this let us look at his physical characterization. **Consider again the various depictions of him (especially on pp. 84, 99 and 106). How does the motif of the man 'without a substance' we have already mentioned get developed? What thematic functions are served by Marlow's depiction of Kurtz as a 'presence'?**

DISCUSSION

Stressing Kurtz as a 'presence' creates both a ghost-story-like sense of suspense and a space, as it were, formerly occupied by Kurtz, that Marlow must fill up with meaning. Extending the 'ghost' simile that I have suggested, I note several other references to Kurtz as a 'presence': an 'initiated wraith' (p. 86) (which incidentally in the original manuscript reads 'ghost'); an 'atrocious phantom' (p. 99); 'a vapour exhaled by the earth' (p. 106); and a Shadow (pp. 105, 107). These occult configurations, 'the living dead', jostle with other closely associated images. Kurtz is seemingly dead: 'a disinterred body' (p. 84), 'an animated image of death carved out of old ivory'

(p. 99); or empty, 'hollow at the core' (p. 97). And against all this overwhelming sense of physical insubstantiality and death stands the emphatically recalled fullness of his 'deep voice' (pp. 99, 102) and 'magnificent eloquence'.

Several theme-clusters attaching to Kurtz seem to me to be suggested here by these physical descriptions. All reveal Marlow's contradictory reading of Kurtz.

1 Kurtz is 'hollow at the core'. In this he resembles other European 'civilizers' like the 'papier-mâché Mephistopheles' brickmaker, or the corrupt Company manager with 'nothing within him' (p. 50). This suggests Marlow is essentially lumping Kurtz together with those European 'shams' who have no moral and psychological 'restraints' with which to resist the temptations, corruptions and excesses Europeans are stereotypically exposed to in 'darkest Africa'. With Kurtz in this role, the voice might echo loudly and meaninglessly, as empty vessels are wont to do, and it receives Marlow's contempt.

2 Kurtz is like one of the infernal Shades from classical mythology. These figures inhabited the underworld but were unable to find peace, compulsively telling any stray mortal who happened upon them their sorry stories. Kurtz, too, is a 'shadow', a 'wandering and tormented thing' (p. 107).

3 Kurtz, as 'an image of death carved out of old ivory' and discoursing to the 'savages', seemed to me to anticipate Kurtz's death-bed 'ivory face' (p. 111). In *that* context, like the proverbial drowning man whose whole life flashes momentarily before him, Kurtz perhaps lived 'his life again in every detail of desire, temptation and surrender'. Then the voice, correspondingly, would not be empty or as sounding brass, nor necessarily compulsive, but rather the full articulation of wisdom in 'that supreme moment of complete knowledge'.

4 Kurtz's presence as a ghost figure after his actual death comes to haunt at least Marlow's imagination. By a paradoxical process of transference it then might seem as if the 'presence' compels *Marlow* to repeat Kurtz's story to others, to become, so to speak, his voice. Transference certainly seems suggested on board the *Nellie* when we are told that Marlow, sitting apart from his listeners in the darkness, 'had been no more to us than a voice' (p. 58).

Other elements of depiction may have struck you and perhaps suggested thematic configurations. For example, the image of Kurtz, assaulted by the powers of darkness, who had 'made a bargain for his soul with the devil' (p. 85) associates him with Faust, for whom anything and everything was justified if his mind is enlarged. In this Faustian capacity, of course, he directly *contradicts* that of 1 above. He's not of the company of papier-mâché Mephistopheles now. Rather, he has flung himself into the arms of a 'real' devil – the wilderness.

In summary, the mutually contradictory readings of Kurtz that Marlow offers have him functioning simultaneously as an empty European sham *and* a remarkable man fully articulating a wisdom bought at the expense of living in extremis. Marlow is unable to impose a consistent meaning on him, and consequently Kurtz's voice, too, is profoundly ambivalent.

Why, to take up our earlier question, is Marlow so haunted by Kurtz's voice, particularly when on his own admission he has not yet heard his 'splendid monologues'? Has he got the idea from what others in the Company have said? In considering this, you might look also at the actual speech of Kurtz which is *quoted*. How much of it is there in the novel? Would you describe it as remarkable for its eloquence? (Consider p. 102, for instance.)

DISCUSSION

In the versions of Kurtz others have given Marlow, it is Kurtz's 'superior' *material* achievements and power that have been the source of gossip and envy. Nothing has been said about his talk. Moreover, and much more important, very little of Kurtz's speech is quoted verbatim. Most of it comes second-hand, filtered through Marlow's interpretative representation. What *is* cited I would describe as abrupt, egocentric, and terse – hardly the 'noble' and 'lofty' discourse which Marlow sees it as. Again, reading against the grain, the narrative tells us more than Marlow wishes. Furthermore, although the narration (quoted above, p. 89) creates the impression that Marlow, in the act of utterance, suddenly achieves a moment of self-knowledge – 'I made the strange discovery that I had never imagined him as doing, you know, but as discoursing' (p. 83) – in fact, he contradicts what he has already told us. Wasn't his first real sense of Kurtz precisely his picturing him 'turning his back suddenly on the headquarters' (p. 62)? Just as then Marlow had good need and reason to 'see' Kurtz as an ally and project his own interests on to him, so now, the new and emphatic centering on Kurtz's voice and eloquence answers another need. Marlow, confronting the 'meaningless' wilderness, seeks an audible and comprehensible voice to explain it. He is ready to endow Kurtz's voice (in one of its contradictory functions at least) with that power and authority.

(iv) The Uses of Speech

Marlow's emphasis also serves a central Conradian preoccupation: the theme of language. This theme, which we have seen closely connected to the political critique in earlier chapters (especially Chapter 4), now re-emerges as a concern for the functions of the human voice. **To locate these functions generally, and to recognize the ambivalences in Kurtz's voice specifically, look at the following quotations. They define the idea of the human voice, sometimes Kurtz's, sometimes others', in relation to a broader context. How is the voice identified? What does it stand in contrast to?**

(a) . . . the great river I could see through a sombre gap glittering, as it flowed broadly by without a murmur. All this was great, expectant, mute, while the man jabbered about himself. I wondered whether the stillness on the face of the immensity looking at us two were meant as an appeal or as a menace. What were we who had strayed in here? Could we handle that dumb thing, or would it handle us? I felt how big, how confoundedly big, was that thing that couldn't talk, and perhaps was deaf as well.   (p. 56)

(b) All this talk [of the Manager's] seemed to me so futile . . . I flung out of his hut . . . muttering to myself my opinion of him. He was a chattering idiot.   (pp. 51–2)

(c) 'Try to be civil, Marlow,' growled a voice, and I knew there was at least one listener awake besides myself.   (p. 67)

(d) An appeal to me in this fiendish row – is there? Very well; I hear; I admit, but I have a voice, too, and for good or evil mine is the speech that cannot be silenced. Of course, a fool, what with sheer fright and fine sentiments is always safe. Who's that grunting? (p. 69)

(e) they shouted periodically together strings of amazing words that resembled no sounds of human language; and the deep murmurs of the crowd, interrupted suddenly, were like the responses of some satanic litany. . . . There was an eddy in the mass of human bodies, and the woman with helmeted head and tawny cheeks rushed out to the very brink of the stream. She put out her hands, shouted something, and all that wild mob took up the shout in a roaring chorus of articulated, rapid, breathless utterance.

'Do you understand this?' I asked.

He kept on looking out past me with fiery longing eyes, with a mingled expression of wistfulness and hate. He made no answer, but I saw a smile, a smile of indefinable meaning, appear on his colourless lips that a moment after twitched convulsively. 'Do I not?' he said slowly, gasping, as if the words had been torn out of him by a supernatural power.   (p. 109)

(f) I think it had whispered to him things about himself which he did not know, things of which he had no conception till he took counsel with this great solitude – and the whisper had proved irresistibly fascinating. It echoed loudly within him because he was hollow at the core . . .   (p. 97)

(g) I've been telling you what we said – repeating the phrases we pronounced – but what's the good? They were common everyday words – the familiar, vague sounds exchanged on every waking day of life. But what of that? They had behind them, to my mind, the terrific suggestiveness of words heard in dreams, of phrases spoken in nightmares.   (pp. 107–8)

DISCUSSION

Within the broad range of kinds of utterance which these passages exemplify, there is, I think, a sort of economy of speech and silence. Clear, articulate speech is juxtaposed to two other sorts: barely audible or sensible *chatter* and frenzied noise. But these utterances are also defined in relation to the silence of the wilderness. Look at the synonyms for speech and silence which the excerpts exploit. How are they distributed – that is, which human agents are given which attributes of speech?

In general, the human voice is variously described as 'talk', 'jabber', 'chatter', 'grunt', 'gasp', 'whisper', and 'murmur'. (There are, of course, other synonyms not appearing here.) It is only the humans who inhabit the wilderness who don't so much talk as make a 'fiendish row' and a 'roaring chorus'. Theirs is an incomprehensible, barely articulate, non-human noise. (We have already made reference to the cultural politics of this specific representation in the previous chapter.)

Those associated with the Company – and, quite as important, the listeners on the *Nellie* with the exception of the framing narrator – tend to have their talk described in derogatory terms: 'jabber', 'chatter', 'growls'. We might recognize the association of such words with animal ejaculations, but in this case the talk is 'futile' (gossiping, complaining) rather than incomprehensible. In any case, it is a speech oblivious of the silence of the wilderness and the appealing 'noise' of its inhabitants.

We have seen already how much the brooding stillness of the wild and the 'frenzy' of the natives both frightens and intrigues Marlow, who seeks for an intelligible translation of their meaning. He is looking for a voice which can articulate it. But in his own case (example (d)), his voice is defined as a controlling defence against, a resistance to, the wilderness and its call. His is a clear voice all right (not jabber or chatter). However, in its very syntax, it is a voice in opposition ('but I have a voice, too') – in opposition both to the appealing mystery of the frenzy *and* to the grunting interjection of his 'civilized' audience.

If Marlow nevertheless desires articulation of this mysterious brooding, it is perhaps not surprising that he *anticipates* in Kurtz a voice which will fit the bill. His is the voice Marlow *needs*, in order to transmit the meanings of the incomprehensible frenzy. Paradoxically then, according to my reading, for all Kurtz's alleged eloquence, he does not master his own voice but is, rather, the amplification of the 'whisper' of the wilderness. This wilderness speaks through him – 'as if the words had been torn out of him by a supernatural power' – and its unspeakableness (in both senses) is given utterance. Unlike Marlow, whose voice is some sort of self-defence against the wild (see quotation d), Kurtz cannot master it, try as he will ('Oh but I will wring your heart yet!').

As we have already noticed and as passage (g) illustrates, there is a stark discrepancy between what Kurtz actually says and the meanings Marlow *inscribes* in the words he utters. Kurtz doesn't in fact say anything profound; Marlow endows it with profundity. Notice Marlow's acknowledgement of this interpreting subjectivity in such phrases as 'I was convinced', 'to my mind'. For Marlow, the authority for this lies in Kurtz's position. Marlow's seeing Kurtz as living at the very limits of experience – of the social and of the mortal – makes his words *mean* so much more.

Look again at how Marlow's narrative convinces us that Kurtz, struggling back to his followers, does indeed live at the very limits. This 'culminating point' portrays Kurtz in what for Marlow is surely his primary function: he rejects this known world by exceeding its limits and experiencing existence over the threshold:

> I tried to break the spell – the heavy, mute spell of the wilderness – that seemed to draw him to its pitiless breast by the awakening of forgotten and brutal instincts, by the memory of gratified and monstrous passions. This alone, I was convinced, had driven him out to the edge of the forest, to the bush, towards the gleam of fires, the throb of drums, the drone of weird incantations; this alone had beguiled his unlawful soul beyond the bounds of permitted aspirations. And, don't you see, the terror of the position was not in being knocked on the head – though I had a very lively sense of that danger, too – but in this, that I had to deal with a being to whom I could not appeal in the name of anything high or low. I had, even like the niggers, to invoke him – himself – his own exalted and incredible degradation. There was nothing either above or below him, and I knew it. He had kicked himself loose of the earth. Confound the man! he had kicked the very earth to pieces. He was alone, and I before him did not know whether I stood on the ground or floated in the air.   (p. 107)

What do you understand by the 'bounds of permitted aspirations'? And if Kurtz is transgressing them, who, in the novel, lives within them?

DISCUSSION

The phrase suggests to me a spatial economy equivalent to the economy of speech which I alluded to earlier. For Marlow, it seems, there is the known and contained social world of the community, the civilized European community; and there is a space beyond it ungoverned by its rules, norms or forms of knowledge. The first is structured and coheres through the exercise of law and other social conventions. A bourgeois world at home in the language of law and gossip, it is pre-eminently inhabited by the likes of Marlow's audience on the *Nellie*, and by extension, we may take it, Conrad's readers. A fuller articulation of this occurs on page 85. Note there the references to the social function of language to order and legislate this space ('whispering' (!) of public opinion). This world certainly knows criminality and occasions of moral turpitude, of course. In this respect the Company agents, even if corrupt, self-seeking, and gossipy, belong to it. They do not challenge or refute its terms; on the contrary, butchery and greed are merely the obverse side of a familiar coin. In his function as hollow sham Kurtz is of this world, too, and he is located *within* it by those back in the sepulchral city who 'know' him as a 'remarkable man' – for they can imagine or know of no other world. But Marlow can and has. Remember his first powerful image of Kurtz *turning away* from the Company Central Station, a figure which is now repeated in Kurtz crawling away from the steamer back into the jungle. Figuratively it articulates what for Marlow is Kurtz's chief importance: he's turned his back and embraced the darkness. Nothing joins Kurtz to the known social world any longer, which is why Marlow can make no appeal to him, to re-attach him, within its terms – high or low, moral or selfish. Those restraining qualities which Marlow has identified in work and through which he maintains himself within limits while recognizing the existence of what these limits cannot contain – it is these restraints Kurtz has renounced. Work, or to put it metonymically, rivets, are what Marlow wants, 'and [they] were what really Mr Kurtz wanted if he had only known it' (p. 59). So unattached by rivets (or what they can stand for), Kurtz crosses the threshold into that other atavistic space of 'monstrous passions' and 'unspeakable rites' which the wilderness, *for Marlow*, embodies. This final emphasis is important. We saw in the last chapter how certain cultural stereotypes which Marlow employs generate interpretative meanings. Now – and Marlow almost admits it – he is projecting on to Kurtz's actions and 'common everyday words' meanings which he needs them to carry if indeed he images him as being at or beyond the limits.

(v) The Meaning of the Cry

Literal turning points and thresholds, returns and boundary cross-
ings, are powerful figures in Marlow's thinking – his journey to
Kurtz and thus his story is motivated exclusively by one. The same
figure, I would suggest, is central to Conrad's imagination, too:
Marlow's tale is being told on the *Nellie* at a point of suspension,
while all on board are waiting for the tide to turn. The ultimate
boundary is of course that between life and death, and this, for
Marlow, endows Kurtz's words with their supreme authority. Not
only is he speaking for that other, the silent wilderness; he is uttering
judgement just this side of the final silence.

Kurtz seems to epitomize what Walter Benjamin has described
as the story-teller's essential authority:

> It is, however, characteristic that not only a man's knowledge or
> wisdom, but above all his real life – and this is the stuff that stories are
> made of – first assumes transmissible form at the moment of his death.
> Just as a sequence of images is set in motion inside a man as his life
> comes to an end – unfolding the views of himself under which he has
> encountered himself without being aware of it – suddenly in his
> expressions and looks the unforgettable emerges and imparts to
> everything that concerned him that authority which even the poorest
> wretch in dying possesses for the living around him. This authority is
> at the very source of the story. Death is the sanction of everything that
> the storyteller can tell. He has borrowed his authority from death.[3]

That Kurtz can transmit to Marlow an articulation and judgement
on his experience at the limit, that he can turn experience into a voice,
a story, is what for Marlow guarantees him his 'moral victory'. But
what is the substance of this judgement? How are his repeated last
words to be interpreted? Marlow calls it a summing-up, and any
familiarity with literary death-bed confessions would lead us to
anticipate at this point a final resolution of the ambiguities and
enigmas we have been confronting. So what does 'The horror! The
horror!' actually *mean*?

Not surprisingly, the words have received more critical commentary than any other (fictional) famous last words. Some critics
have found them heroically affirmative, others desperately nihilistic.
Here are some specific critical responses:

Lionel Trilling sees in Kurtz the epitome of the modern hero:

> It is one of the great points of Conrad's story that Marlow speaks of
> the primitive life of the jungle not as being noble or charming or even
> free but as being base and sordid – and for that reason compelling: he
> himself feels quite overtly its dreadful attraction. It is to this devilish
> baseness that Kurtz has yielded himself, and yet Marlow, although he

does indeed treat him with hostile irony, does not find it possible to suppose that Kurtz is anything but a hero of the spirit. For me it is still ambiguous whether Kurtz's famous deathbed cry, 'The horror! The horror!' refers to the approach of death or to his experience of savage life. Whichever it is, to Marlow the fact that Kurtz could utter this cry at the point of death, while Marlow himself, when death threatens him, can know it only as weary greyness, marks the difference between the ordinary man and a hero of the spirit. Is this not the essence of the modern belief about the nature of the artist, the man who goes down into that hell which is the historical beginning of the human soul, a beginning not outgrown but established in humanity as we know it now, preferring the reality of this hell to the bland lies of the civilization that has overlaid it?[4]

Jacques Berthoud pushes this notional heroism further:

Problematic as the further meaning of Kurtz's cry has proved, there are two things that can be confidently said about it. The first is that it records some sort of 'ultimate truth' about man; the second is that it implies that this truth is morally abhorrent. . . . It is only in his relation to Kurtz that Marlow might be taken for the ordinary man; in relation to everyone else in the story he represents surely, the moral man. For him, the dual reality revealed by the test of the jungle poses a problem of conduct: in its aspect of primitive truth, it demands his courage, for it has to be outfaced; in its form of civilized goal it requires his fidelity, for it has to be upheld. For Kurtz, on the other hand, this duality is not so much something to be dealt with, as something to be embodied or enacted. He *is*, on his death-bed, the horror he perceives. His last cry, like that of Faustus, is the cry of a man who can only learn what his soul is worth as he discovers that it is irretrievably lost, or of one who can only affirm moral value as he perceives that it cannot exist. If Marlow is the moral hero, Kurtz becomes, for a visionary instant, the tragic hero.[5]

But in contrast, and re-emphasizing the reading of Kurtz as a hollow sham, Douglas Brown sees Marlow at this point as so fatally fascinated by Kurtz's rhetoric that his own moral categories are desperately disturbed:

It seems perverse and sentimental to attribute to anyone except Marlow the notion that Kurtz represents a character to be admired, or his end some sort of 'moral victory': a Marlow, moreover, recording the disorder and fascination remembered from a state of nervous collapse. Yet a good deal of criticism appears to suppose simply this to be Conrad's own view of the matter.[6]

Finally, a view which releases Marlow from all complicity; that of Ian Watt:

But the main object of Kurtz's condemnation is surely himself, and what he has done; his dying whisper pronounces rejection of the Faustian compact with the wilderness which had 'sealed his soul to its own'. . . . His final cry can only be judged, as Marlow judges it, 'an affirmation, a moral victory' . . . , if it constitutes an acknowledgement of the horror of his former deeds. [. . . Critics like Trilling] ignore the disavowals which both Marlow and Conrad made of any admiration for Kurtz. Marlow's overt judgments are unremittingly hostile or ironic: 'Mr Kurtz was no idol of mine' . . . , he affirms; and in this, as we have seen, Marlow reflects Conrad's intentions. The fact [is] that both Conrad and Marlow overtly dissociate themselves from sharing or admiring Kurtz's satanism.[7]

How far do you disagree with any of these views?

DISCUSSION

Although I find points to agree with in all of them – the Faust allusions (Berthoud and Watt), Marlow's state of mind (Brown), Marlow's ambivalence towards the awful jungle (Trilling), for instance – all of them in my view show too ready a willingness to slide over profound difficulties with the episode. Consequently they confidently succumb to a univalent meaning and a unequivocal judgement, which – in the metaphor of the novel's opening – delivers them the kernel of the story. True, Trilling and Berthoud do acknowledge the 'problematic', 'ambiguous' nature of Kurtz's cry, but not for long. They conclude with a resounding 'ultimate truth' about mankind (which soon loses its inverted commas). They, heroically, embrace Kurtz's 'tragic heroism'. For Brown this is unambiguously perverse, and for Watt, who has managed to erase all of Marlow's admiration for Kurtz, Marlow at least is unequivocally sanitized of Kurtz's satanism, perverse or not.

In brief – and perhaps this is true of *any* reading, including mine – all the interpretations seem to discover the Kurtz, and by extension the Marlow, that they want to find there. In this they paradoxically resemble Marlow, whose Kurtz is endowed with all the (contradictory) meanings Marlow inscribes in him. My own alternative is not so much to offer a competing conclusive judgement, but rather to outline my difficulties and doubts about Marlow's account and the meaning of Kurtz's cry and 'moral victory'. Let me start with Kurtz's words themselves.

First, I noted a destabilizing irony about the delivery of the words. As a verbal utterance they are whispered, 'a cry no more than a breath' – the closest form to inarticulacy and non-utterance which Kurtz's 'eloquence' achieves. It is itself almost literally 'unspeakable'. As a final pronouncement upon 'all the wisdom, and all truth, and all sincerity', it is peculiarly indefinite in its reference and its context. What, for example, is its tone? Is it uttered in terror, amazed repulsion, or appalled desire? Marlow seems to *contrast* it with 'a word of careless contempt' (p. 113) – but isn't that precisely what it is?

Second, what does the cry actually *refer* to? Is Kurtz, on his death-bed, looking back over his own past experience and delivering a horrified moral judgement on it? That could be called a 'moral victory', but then it would be in the name of civil values after all. Alternatively, is Kurtz seeing in himself a vision of *all* human nature? If so, he would be condemning not just himself but all humanity, in which case civilization would be declared a sham. Or is 'all the universe' the subject of the cry? This might render humanity not so much morally abhorrent as irrelevant and trivial. And what if the tone is one of appalled *desire*? If the glimpsed truth has 'the strange commingling of desire and hate', the 'horror' would mean something Kurtz wished to embrace. How would that be a 'moral victory'? Or would the full *recognition* of the desire in its awfulness (rather than its defeat) constitute a victory? An odd sort of 'moral victory', where Kurtz can resist anything but temptation!

I do not have clear answers to these questions. I do not think the text authoritatively provides them. This would mean that at the very moment when the narrative appears to deliver the promised center-ing meaning, that meaning has been denied or at the very least deferred. We thought we were dealing with an apricot, with a solid non-contradictory kernel of truth and in fact we've been peeling an onion.

In a review of Conrad's *Notes on Life and Letters* (1921), E. M. Forster delivered himself of a famous remark appropriate here. Conrad's essays, he complained, 'do suggest that he is misty in the middle as well as at the edges, that the secret casket of his genius contains a vapour rather than a jewel'.[8] Forster's complaint is both perceptive and, I would say, wrong. He thinks (his metaphor implies) that there is a truth inside, in the casket, the kernel, which Conrad fails to deliver. My point is that that notion of truth is precisely what the narrative deliberately frustrates and denies. At the core of the novel lies an absence (an absent truth) which confirms what the framing narrator warned us of in Marlow's yarns (p. 30). For all Marlow's talk of his 'candour' and 'conviction' (p. 113), Kurtz's cry, accordingly, would be a parody or mock version of Benjamin's truthful, death-bed storytelling.

(vi) Marlow's Intended

After this false end, not surprisingly, lie other false ends. Marlow on his return to Europe acts as the vehicle and voice of Kurtz's story, just as Kurtz has acted for the voice of the wilderness.

The interview with Kurtz's Intended is the last of several which

Marlow has in the sepulchral city. Look again at those interviews (pp. 114–20) and note any similarities they bear to one another.

DISCUSSION

I noticed how in each case Marlow's visitor claimed to 'know' Kurtz. Each has his or her own story of Kurtz's greatness, and each wants to hear Marlow confirm it. An official, a fellow 'calling himself Kurtz's cousin', a journalist and finally Kurtz's Intended all have their versions of Kurtz, narratives appropriate (and appropriating Kurtz) to their concerns.

Furthermore, they all want something from Marlow; he has to pass something on to them from Kurtz. Literally, that something is a possession of his; metaphorically, it is their image of him. In each case, also, their claim to 'know' Kurtz is subjected to Marlow's acerbic irony. When he records their statements about Kurtz – 'How that man could talk', 'He was an – an – extremist' – and assents to them, not one is free of an ironic, blackly comic, reading. For as voyeur and part-actor in Kurtz's psychic striptease, Marlow has gone at least to the edge of the threshold Kurtz has crossed and so can claim an authority to a knowledge they cannot even conceive. But Marlow does not transmit *that* fact to them. Rather, he is complicit in their rehabilitating of Kurtz, their domesticating reconstruction of him.

This is no more clearly evident than in his meeting with the Intended and the version of Kurtz's story he transmits to her. What he passes on is the capacity to regenerate illusions, fictions, about Kurtz.

Look at the final encounter (pp. 117–21). Note the uses made of the apparition motif again. Do you discern any notable similarities with that earlier 'apparition', Kurtz's savage mistress?

DISCUSSION

An almost disembodied figure, pale and ghostly against a black background, the Intended is portrayed by Marlow as 'floating towards [him]' as if in suspension, outside concrete time and place. Reminiscent of the French symbolist Odilon Redon's fantasy portraits, physically she is all but an ethereal unreality. Like Kurtz's 'savage mistress', she is an apparition of haunting beauty, but while the former is (according to ethnic stereotype) black and all-sexual Amazonian physicality, the Intended is non-sexual spirituality and innocence. Marlow sees both of them as not quite of *this* world: they inhabit either a prehistoric or an ahistoric one. (In neither case does the woman exist in history.) As women, both are Other. The apparition-like Intended is a phantasmagoria, a space for the imagination, to be filled with meanings. She is Civilized Woman, just as Kurtz's mistress is Savage Woman. Twin-like, the two share a tragic fidelity to the male, as underlined by their identical embracing arm gestures. Simultaneously, as imaginative spaces, they can be endowed with contradictory qualities. Conrad, as the creator of this narrative situation, has distributed contrasting 'female' traits between them: knowledge/innocence, sexuality/spirituality. This distribution holds intact sexist and ethnocentric categories of women which, in their crudest form, emerge as the savage-whore/civilized-madonna stereotypes. Ideological constructions have no difficulty with contradictions: the Other is a space large enough to hold any anxieties, fears, prejudices and desires. The configuration has been implicit in earlier depictions of the European women living in 'that beautiful world of their own' (pp. 39, 84). Marlow's depiction and Conrad's narrative construction allow us then to see the black woman metonymically as standing for that space in which Kurtz has enacted all those unspeakable rites and exercised those monstrous passions. Conversely, the Intended is a metonym not just for European womankind, but more generally for the idealizing aspect of 'civilization'. She represents what Conrad has been at pains to demonstrate about one feature of civilization: it is a self-confirming space inhabited by the butcher and the policeman, the listeners on the *Nellie* and the readers, all of whom, according to the argument, construct self-protective illusions which fend off their own (now re-distributed) passions.

Coming when it does in the narrative, with all the admittedly melodramatic focus it receives, Marlow's lie carries a profound charge, then. It has already been anticipated in the narrative – in the references to Marlow's loathing of the lie, smacking of mortality, and most prominently in his interruption of narrative flow to mention the Intended (p. 84). This narrative disturbance, this temporal fracture with a return to the present on the *Nellie*, seems quite unmotivated; its jagged rhythms imply a degree of energetic repression of guilt at having told the lie. Arguably, his lying about Kurtz's story has now generated Marlow's need to tell it, if not *straight* at least *again*.

So Marlow lies when he says, 'Your name'. So what's in a name? **Does 'Your name' tell us some sort of truth after all? Do you think some other lying, dying words would have done? Imagine, for example, Marlow had said Kurtz's last words were, 'Let others, now, bring light to the darkness!' Would that, as a lie, have made much difference?**

DISCUSSION

My sense is that they might have *done*, but not told us so much. First, his lie is the melodramatic, romantically conventional closure to the official love story of Kurtz that the Intended wants to hear and has constructed for Marlow to utter. If there are tears in the nature of things, at least this end justifies the waiting and the love. The irony with which this closure is treated by Marlow (the heavens do not fall) marks one major departure from the nineteenth-century romance that the novel has shadowed. Second, as a proper name, it blatantly contradicts the unspeakable, that is the unnameable, experience or knowledge to which 'the horror' makes reference. That which is unutterable, beyond the resources of language fully to express, has been mockingly transformed into the transmissible *name*. But there is a further ironic sleight-of-hand here. The very words 'your name' really *conceal* the named identity of the Intended – as 'Kurtz said, "Gretchen"' would not have done. So with her actual identity left undisclosed, we know her only as someone defined by Kurtz's *intention* of marriage. Perhaps this indicates the most important function of 'your name'. Marlow's particular lie implies a gesture on Kurtz's part – if not exactly a *promise* to her (after all, he *is* dying) at least the *desire* to love and marry her. So the words are a token, reinforcing the image of socially acceptable union and continuity. 'Your name', in this sense, is a metonym for social and sexual relations which embody order, coherence and civilized reproduction of the same. Marlow passes on to the Intended the image of marital continuity. Of course, this is only an image, an illusion: Kurtz is by now dead. But her ideal of the two of them remains intact and with it the social, moral and sexual values this ideal endorses – and which Kurtz's actual experience (as interpreted, rendered and transmitted by Marlow to his audience) has done everything to undermine and deconstruct. Through Marlow's lie continuity displaces discontinuity.

Why does he lie? Is it because women cannot take the strain of unpleasant truths? Perhaps. The male construction of the black lover and the Intended may propose this sexist view. **But look more closely at Marlow's characterization of 'their beautiful world' and the context in which these comments come. (Look back at Chapter 3, pp. 33–5, for this.) Are they straightforwardly chauvinist?**

(a) It's queer how out of touch with truth women are. They live in a world of their own, and there had never been anything like it, and never can be. It is too beautiful altogether, and if they were to set it up it would go to pieces before the first sunset. Some confounded fact we men have been living contentedly with ever since the day of creation would start up and knock the whole thing over. (p. 39)

(b) 'I laid the ghost of his gifts at last with a lie,' he began, suddenly. 'Girl! What? Did I mention a girl? Oh, she is out of it. We must help them to stay in that beautiful world of their own, lest ours gets worse. Oh, she had to be out of it.'   (p. 84)

DISCUSSION

Passage (a) does seem to me to reinforce a 'manly' view of 'womanly' other-worldly self-delusion. It is a specifically Victorian cultural construction: women can live as angels immune from the wicked male world. But in the context of the narrative, it comes just after Marlow's interview with the Company boss and the doctor. Marlow is feeling distinctly complicit and awkward when, conversing with his aunt, he is allied with the march of progress. Suddenly he gets irritated. His apparently confident talk of a male community – 'we men' – has been completely belied by what has preceded it. He by no means shares all their assumptions. In other words, moral and political embarrassment on Marlow's part is *displaced* onto a stereotypic and easy target – women's folly, and in a grand gesture of false consciousness, male solidarity can be once again belatedly claimed. Marlow's account of his up-river experiences, of course, provokes a lot of disparaging remarks about the 'fools' who inhabit the city of solid pavements, butchers and policemen – that is, his male audience. Perhaps (a) implies men can live with contradictory facts *too* contentedly. Certainly (b) reveals the real interest in keeping women in their beautiful world: *lest ours gets worse*. Men's comfortable worlds would perhaps be too disturbed. So I would say Marlow is both complicit in and yet knowingly *reveals* his chauvinism, at least to the audience. These narrative disturbances tell us a great deal about the problematic claims to a shared narrative and social community.

One final question about the lie: is it a lie at all? If, according to some interpretations (though I have indicated my sense of ambivalence), 'The horror' *does* refer to a knowledge on Kurtz's part of civilization's capacity for hypocrisy and self-delusion, then part of this horror would be precisely the conventionality of social relations represented by the Intended. If so, then 'your name' would be a synonym for the horror, not a lie. What do you think?

The lie does not bring down the heavens. For all the melodrama of the style and setting in this scene, the fact that it was a 'trifle' parodies rather than reinforces the conventional novelistic end of revelatory monumental truths. Is Kurtz's 'wisdom' still hollower than we thought? Nothing much happens anyway. Marlow's voice peters out into a darkness like the darkness his lie has fended off.

So, on his return, Marlow is the conscious accomplice of other people's fictions, which maintain civilization's self-deluding practices. Against the horrific insights which Kurtz has *lived*, Marlow's defence is to tell a lie to those 'whose knowledge of life was to [Marlow] an irritating pretence' (p. 113). But lying isn't Marlow's only defence and way out of the darkness.

(vii) The Work of Narration

We have already considered one other: physical work. It is in the immediacy of practical labour that Marlow had discovered 'surface-truth enough . . . to save a wiser man' (p. 70). Work which in so many other ways has been portrayed as exploitative and destructive can, if freely chosen and engaged in, prove a means of self-discovery and protection. It is a form, for Marlow, of kidding on the level: he *knows* (as a would-be wiser man) what it is that work is keeping him in ignorance of. The habits of work enable him to repress his self-awareness:

> 'I got used to it [the wilderness] afterwards; I did not see it any more; I had no time. I had to keep guessing at the channel . . .' (p. 66)

But that consciousness is never *undone*, only channelled. The 'inner truth is hidden', perhaps, by the sublimating effects of work. But *that* fact is not hidden from Marlow's audience, any more than Marlow's lie is: paradoxically, it is a main subject of Marlow's would-be dialogues with them.

With this fact, Conrad engineers one of the profound implications of the novel and reveals a major insight into the nature of the 'civilized': its dual reality. Its capacity perpetually to lie to itself (tell itself stories) for its own self-maintenance, is matched by its capacity to produce (in the cultural sphere, also, of course) other stories which expose the lie and strive to a truthful understanding about it. Civilization (via its cultural forms) can look both ways and usually at the same time.

This suggests there is a *third* form of defence – other than lying or physical work – by which Marlow tackles the darkness: his voice. Consider again the important passage where Marlow acknowledges the fascination of the wilderness:

> An appeal to me in this fiendish row – is there? Very well; I hear; I admit, but I have a voice, too, and for good or evil mine is the speech that cannot be silenced. (p. 69)

Marlow clearly attaches importance to his own voice. But why is the abrupt, almost broken phrasing in the *present tense* (that is, the present of Marlow sitting on the *Nellie*)? 'An appeal to me in this fiendish row – *was* there?' would seem to be more consistent.

The present tense suggests to me that the feeling Marlow *had* is still somehow active and presently effective now, at the time he is narrating. This sense of the *presentness* of past feelings – the haunting motif we have considered – is reinforced elsewhere in *Heart of Darkness* with the surfacing of a troublesome memory. A clear example is his recalling the girl to whom he lied (p. 84). These are experiences that have not been settled.

Marlow's voice *now*, the voice telling the story on board the *Nellie*, is a kind of laborious self-defence. The voice keeps the experience at bay while at the same time articulating it, talking about it. I say 'laborious' intentionally. Marlow's voice, or rather his *act* of telling his experiences, can be seen as a kind of work, a practice. For someone like Conrad, who gave up the profession of seamanship for that of writing, the analogy is by no means outlandish. Recall what Marlow has to say about physical work, and recall, too, those other incidents in the novel which draw attention to the site of narration, to Marlow as storyteller. The following passages provide useful material for comparisons.

(a) 'This simply because I had a notion it somehow would be of help to that Kurtz whom at the time I did not see – you understand. He was just a word for me. I did not see the man in the name any more than you do. Do you see him? Do you see the story? Do you see anything? It seems to me I am trying to tell you a dream – making a vain attempt, because no relation of a dream can convey the dream sensation, that commingling of absurdity, surprise, and bewilderment in a tremor of struggling revolt, that notion of being captured by the incredible which is of the very essence of dreams . . .'

He was silent for a while.

'. . . No, it is impossible; it is impossible to convey the life-sensation of any given epoch of one's existence – that which makes its truth, its meaning – its subtle and penetrating essence. It is impossible. We live, as we dream – alone . . .'

He paused again as if reflecting, then added –

'Of course in this you fellows see more than I could then. You see me, whom you know . . .'

It had become so pitch dark that we listeners could hardly see one another. For a long time already he, sitting apart, had been no more to us than a voice.   (pp. 57–8)

(b) I don't like work – no man does – but I like what is in the work – the chance to find yourself. Your own reality – for yourself, not for others – what no other man can ever know. They can only see the mere show, and never can tell what it really means.   (pp. 59–60)

Telling his story is at times an arduous struggle for Marlow. To make out of the raw material of his life-experience a product – a comprehensible, transmissible story – is as fraught and uncertain as bandaging up the tin-pot boat and plotting a good course. Both activities are somehow provisional, never quite finished. Both have their private meanings for Marlow, and are a process of self-discovery. Putting things into words, trying to find the 'right' words, can itself lead to knowledge. (The clearest example of this is when Marlow recognizes the importance of Kurtz's voice in the act of uttering the words 'talking with Mr Kurtz' (p. 83).) But while the private meanings of the story, of his work, are inaccessible to others, both activities are also pre-eminently *social acts*. Like metaphorical rivets (which, remember, Kurtz could have done with), they join Marlow to an immediate social reality which his dream-like experiences have threatened to disengage him from. To call Marlow's story-telling or his work therapeutic is in no way to belittle them. I think the text strongly suggests – when it does not make explicit – that both activities are ones which he *psychically* needs to engage with. His abrupt and uninvited intervention at the outset of the tale, and his almost oblivious lack of concern for whether anyone is listening to his story, would seem to confirm his need to narrate. Work has a similar psychological function: it can tackle the threat of the wilderness by a displacing attention to surface truths. But over and above this, both activities locate him *socially*, and this, I would suggest, has a self-protective function, too.

Conrad, here, brilliantly anticipates an insight expressed, more theoretically, by Freud in his monograph on *Civilization and Its Discontents* (incidentally, a work worth placing up against *Heart of Darkness* for certain common thematic concerns). In an enticingly brief footnote Freud comments:

> It is not possible, within the limits of a short survey, to discuss adequately the significance of work for the economics of the libido. No other technique for the conduct of life attaches the individual so firmly to reality as laying emphasis on work; for his work at least gives him a secure place in a portion of reality, in the human community. The possibility it offers of displacing a large amount of libidinal components, whether narcissistic, aggressive or even erotic, on to professional work and on to the human relations connected with it lends it a value by no means second to what it enjoys as something indispensable to the preservation and justification of existence in society. Professional activity is a source of special satisfaction if it is a freely chosen one – if, that is to say, by means of sublimation, it makes possible the use of existing inclinations, of persisting or constitutionally reinforced instinctual impulses.[9]

As an abbreviated account of what Kurtz succumbs to, I would proffer this footnote as a profound gloss. It also anchors for me what Marlow perceives in himself and through Kurtz, and what he fends off or manages by his 'monkey-trick' work and his story-telling voice.

Through his work he finds filiation most immediately with the boilermaker (p. 60), the 'savage' fireman (p. 70) and the fine cannibals (p. 67). But his 'monkey-tricks', as he denigratingly calls them (p. 67), are according to Marlow also the common denominator he shares with the others on the *Nellie*. Whether it is plying up the Congo or professing law in London, round the corner from the butcher or policeman (p. 84), work is the common currency. Furthermore, in the lapse between tides, waiting for physical work to resume, directors and accountants of companies are also the audience for his story-telling; they are the immediate social location of his narrative. Their interjections or more often their *implied* interjections occur usually and significantly in response to Marlow's disparaging remarks about monkey-trick work or naïve fools needing no psychological protection. Their interjections suddenly jolt the reader out of the heart of darkness and back into recalling the situation of the narrating act, before a group on board the *Nellie*.

This social dimension of the narration is one of the crucial aspects of Conrad's choice of narrative form. By using a framing narrator to introduce a narrative within a narrative and by identifying an audience for Marlow's story, Conrad foregrounds the very act and condition of narrative. Our attention is thus drawn to the relations between Marlow the experiencer, Marlow the story-teller, and Marlow's listeners. And with Marlow thus foregrounded as narrator, Conrad's own activity as *writer* is self-consciously implicated. How and to what effect does narration take place? The conditions and products of physical work are quickly apparent enough. The boat sails; or the boat sinks. But what about the work of narrative?

In quotation (a) above, Marlow first expresses extreme distrust at the possibility of translating experience into words or narratable form. A romantically solipsistic image of the isolated and imprisoned self is evoked:

'We live, as we dream – alone . . .'

Are we not all prisoners behind our own frontal bones? In some ways Marlow is right. For how *can* we experience another's experience? How can we dream another's dream? The tragedy of untranslatability threatens. We surely are, each of us, unredeemably, only ourselves.

And yet, in the act of *saying* that, Marlow pauses – to reflect, perhaps, upon what he's just said. And he seems to discover something else and pursue a different tack:

'Of course in this you fellows see more than I could then. You see me, whom you know . . .'

This is then immediately and ironically undercut by the framing narrator, who understands it literally. No one can *see* Marlow. But his point surely still holds: you cannot feel and live the experience I have had, but you *may* understand it better than I did living through it, precisely because I have objectified it for you in words and given it the shape of a story, mediating the raw experience in language.

To dream a dream is not to understand it, either. In telling it – to ourselves or a close friend – we may start to. By choosing the particular narrative form he does, Conrad has been able to highlight the relation between experience (the stuff of stories) and understanding. He has thus profoundly questioned any romantic and naïve correlation or coinciding of experience with understanding. And why not? For if the two were necessarily co-existent, all literature, all art, would founder, always, as the second-hand. If an equation of direct experience and understanding held, then art (more specifically the claims of literature), in always coming afterwards, would not even bear/bare the benefits of hindsight.

On the other hand, Conrad is not complacent about narrative securing understanding. The prevarication and self-doubt evident in the quoted passage and its ironic termination in the framing narrator's comment do not indicate a guaranteed act of full communication. True, the framing narrator is alert to the *potentiality* of understanding Marlow's narration, but he may be in a minority of one. He is still waiting, but others may be asleep:

> There was not a word from anybody. The others might have been asleep, but I was awake. I listened, I listened on the watch for the sentence, for the word, that would give me the clue to the faint uneasiness inspired by this narrative that seemed to shape itself without human lips in the heavy night-air of the river. (p. 58)

And if under the conditions of oral story-telling there is still doubt about full understanding, how much more must there be under the conditions of writing. No wonder Conrad was sceptical about the transmissibility of knowledge to a distant, unknown readership. In an oral/aural relationship like Marlow's the audience's presence is confirmed, though even here dialogic *exchange* is held by Conrad to a minimum. In a writerly context, with what confidence can Conrad speak? Who *is* his audience? What meaning and understanding may they glean?

This, we might feel, is where Marlow and Conrad most closely coincide, where the problematics of narration are at issue. Conrad was all too aware of the *work* of creative writing. Talking of 'the creative art of a writer of fiction' in an essay entitled 'Henry James: An Appreciation,' he says:

Action in its essence, the creative art of a writer of fiction may be compared to rescue work carried out in darkness against cross gusts of wind swaying the action of a great multitude. It is rescue work, this snatching of vanishing phases of turbulence, disguised in fair words, out of the native obscurity into a light where the struggling forms may be seen, seized upon, endowed with the only possible form of permanence in this world of relative values – the permanence of memory. And the multitude feels it obscurely too; since the demand of the individual to the artist is, in effect, the cry 'Take me out of myself!' meaning really, out of my perishable activity into the light of imperishable consciousness.[10]

For Conrad writing, the creation of narrative, is a laborious and demanding recuperative task. But the recipients and beneficiaries of this work, the great multitude, are by no means stable and securely anchored. Writing in solitude, to be received and read, *maybe*, in solitude, by individuals possibly distant in space and time – this was not a reassuring mode of communication for Conrad. For a writer, absence and anonymity could only exacerbate the obstacles to understanding which Marlow highlights. In Conrad's case, the imagined fictions seemed often more real than the recipients. His wife Jessie records how on finishing writing *Under Western Eyes* Conrad refused to let her touch the uncorrected manuscript and instead held conversations with the characters he had created, distrusting the reality and reliability of his own wife and doctor.[11] So when, in his famous self-ordinance in the Preface to *The Nigger of the 'Narcissus'* (1897), he says:

My task which I am trying to achieve is, by the power of the written word to make you hear, to make you feel – it is, before all, to make you see[12]

we should register both the *purpose* – of understanding (*seeing*), which Marlow also claims – and also acknowledge the inherent difficulty in this. If he has to *make* us see, success cannot be taken for granted.

With this, let us conclude that Conrad leaves open the question of the possibilities of successful narration and understanding. As my discussion of the major issues of this chapter has, I hope, indicated, I think this is absolutely characteristic of Conradian doubt and scepticism. As my argument about Marlow, the engaged reader and interpreter, has suggested, consciousness may well imply the inescapability of interpretation (the making and transmission of our own meanings). If so, it also implies the impossibility of final and closed meaning.

7. In Lieu of Concluding . . .

In lieu of concluding, Conrad has foregrounded Marlow's problem with truthful story-telling. Highlighting the question of narrative reception and understanding, Conrad's own writerly activity is self-consciously implicated. When Marlow anxiously asks his audience on the *Nellie*, 'Do you see the story? Do you see anything?' the question reverberates for us, as we read, not just as they listen. Like a figure in a picture suddenly addressing the visitors to the gallery, it's as if he were stepping out from a canvas, breaking its frame. We are thus returned to the question of the opening chapter: 'What is it to read? What is the story we are seeing?'

Clearly, by eschewing the framing narration, Conrad could have left the question unasked: not many stories, even those with a first-person narrator, are so explicit about the narrating situation, the act and context of narration. Had he done so, the condition of story-telling and its social meaning for the reader need hardly have registered for us. But this drawing-of-attention to itself, which makes *Heart of Darkness* such a quintessentially modernist work, indicates something central about Conrad's own historical place as a writer. The Double-man, he straddles two territories, negotiating the awkward space between the traditional story-teller and the modern writer, between an oral and a written culture. Friends witness to his marvellous capacity as a raconteur, and the opening image of a familiar community of listeners aboard ship goes to emphasize a cultural nostalgia, a nostalgia, that is, for an immediately knowable and known audience which in the late Victorian period would not have been available to him as a writer. Standing at a historical crux between a moment of narration confident of its audience's shared assumptions and one cut off from it and uncertain of (if not deeply sceptical about) the very existence of such shared truths, Conrad would have been centrally preoccupied with how a story could be told and how, even whether, it could be heard. Such questions become explicit in the form and themes of writing when their answers can no longer be taken for granted. But after all, why else would it be worthwhile posing the questions?

It is no wonder, then, that *Heart of Darkness* has been taken by critics and teachers as a seminal expression of modern literary and cultural concerns. For one of the defining characteristics of modernism can be said to be the self-questioning of the work of art. 'It is self-evident that nothing is self-evident', Adorno has commented on modern art.[1] How true, at all levels of meaning, is this statement for *Heart of Darkness*! Nothing can be taken for granted. The novel marks a very early example of the sustained attention which Conrad was to pay to the problematics and self-reflectivity of fiction. This can be seen at work in all his major fiction, from *Lord Jim* (1900) and *Nostromo* (1904) through *The Secret Agent* (1907) and preeminently in *Under Western Eyes* (1910), as well as in the shorter but no less powerful 'The Secret Sharer' (1910) and *The Shadow-Line* (1916). At times in his writing career Conrad was to sound very confident about his capacity to mould his narrative to achieve a level of communication bordering on the visionary, a task set in his preface to *The Nigger of the 'Narcissus'*, which I have already discussed.[2] In 'A Familiar Preface' to *A Personal Record* he talks of 'the force of words' to affect 'a whole mass of lives'. Powerful words, rather than thoughtful reflection, are the route to men's souls: 'Give me the right word and the right accent and I will move the world'.[3] But forever the double man, Conrad simultaneously undercuts this confident assertion about unity of speaker, word, and receiver. Even as he was writing *Heart of Darkness*, he was also working on *Lord Jim*, in which Marlow again appears. Here, less the actor this time than the mediating narrator of another's adventure, Marlow contests the possibility of resolution and the assurance of telling the truth:

> [Jim] existed for me and after all it is only through me that he exists for you. [. . . But] the last word is not said – probably shall never be said. Are not our lives too short for that full utterance which through all our stammerings is of course our only and abiding intention? I have given up expecting those last words, whose ring, if they could only be pronounced would shake both heaven and earth. There is never time to say our last word – the last word of our love, of our desire, faith, remorse, submission, revolt. The heaven and the earth must not be shaken, I suppose – at least not by us who know so many truths about either. My last words about Jim shall be few. I affirm he had achieved greatness; but the thing would be dwarfed in the telling, or rather the hearing. Frankly it is not my words that I mistrust but your minds. I could be eloquent were I not afraid you fellows have starved your imaginations to feed your bodies. (*Lord Jim*, pp. 171–2)

Much can be gained from thinking about *Heart of Darkness* in relation to *Lord Jim* – not least in comparing the two figures of Marlow, the roles of Jim and Kurtz both as insiders ('one of us') and as 'heroic' outsiders, and the representation of the European confronting the exotic Other. Let it suffice here to note two central concerns: doubts about language and utterance, and even greater doubts about the receiving imagination and comprehending capacity of the audience/reader. *Heart of Darkness* is an early and profound reflection on this modernist crisis of language and communication.

I think these doubts can be traced in several textual 'disturbances' in *Heart of Darkness*. The work of 'deconstructive' critics like Derrida has shown how useful it can be to attend to the so-called 'marginal' features of texts. Reading them against the grain – against the terms and values which ostensibly govern the work – often reveals that they are 'symptomatic' of contradictory tensions within it. The thrust of this critical position is to undermine a 'phonocentric' view of the literary work, the idea that the written work is the transcription of the living voice of its creator. According to this idea, the author is in full self-possession and able to communicate his inner being and intention through masterly control of language, which is his willing and obedient tool. Implicit in this view is a belief in a non-contradictory, knowable, coherent self and a confidence in language as a 'natural' (or transparent and ideologically undetermined) medium of expression. Such claims deconstructive critics would contest. For them, the text should not be thought of as the site of authorially possessed meaning; indeed the characteristic word 'text' suggests something less personally immediate than 'novel' or 'writing' implies. Instead, odd stylistic traits – a troublesome turn of phrase, a recurrent but minor motif – can then be seen to cast a critical and destabilizing light on what presents itself as seamless and coherent.[4]

Paradoxically, Conrad may have less argument with this position than might at first appear, given that he gave up an honest living as a sailor, and thought of himself as a writer, who might have had a vested interest in the notion of authorial control. For as is so evident, *Heart of Darkness* does not reveal much confidence or complacency about the status of Marlow's story-telling and its grasp on meaning or about the innocence of language. Like other documents of literary modernism, Conrad's work identifies and anticipates many of the concerns later theoretical expositions have articulated. Theory arises out of troubled practice. And Marlow's practice, let alone Conrad's, is troubled enough for the novel to raise as explicit thematic issues what later become theoretical, conceptual questions: the search for and problematics of the voice; the status and seductions of the written and the spoken; the critique of political and cultural representations; doubts about ultimate meanings (currently termed by 'deconstructionists' the 'transcendental signifier'). But it is Marlow's 'actual' experiences and confrontations which provoke these questions, to which I have lent abstract formulation. They spring out of his and Conrad's immediate history. To call *Heart of Darkness* a post-modernist text before its time is both to patronize (how clever of it to be up with us!) and to miss the historical point I have tried to stress.[5] The work is a work in and of its time, and the fault-lines in its structure record a particular historical and cultural moment. Without wishing to endorse a simple view of the biographical Conrad as authorizing all its significations, I would nevertheless argue that his authorial functions – in part creator (but never *ex nihilo*), in part seismograph, in part a refracting lens of consciousness transforming as it receives – all entail a historically circumscribed entity, and at least partially imply a self-conscious insertion into and inscribing of history.

So without stressing 'deconstruction', my approach has sought to encourage you in reading the texture of the novel against the grain, which can mean simply reading as sensitively and questioningly as you can. Worrying at 'turbulences' can thus prove productive. Trivial or minute as such stylistic aberrations may seem, they signal real crux points. They are not just problems of style. Indeed, in Conrad at least, very few stylistic problems are. They are moments in the text which can, as it were, embarrass it into revealing more than it thought it did. Marlow's very first words, 'And this also . . .' which I asked you to ponder in Chapter 2 (pp. 20–1), signal precisely a tension between the narrative's status as oral or written. In its implied continuity with the foregoing sentences – a continuity which can only exist at the level of the written, not the spoken, because the framing narrator has not been speaking – the ontological status of the text (its source and destination) remains quite unclear. The fact that we easily read over it and accept (or fail to notice) the writerly sleight-of-hand attests to our comfortable assumptions about the colloquial/known community of the oral situation. But at the same time, the fact that the continuity can exist only on the page, not on the boat deck, points to the very problem of community understanding and social continuity that the novel explores and contests as one of its central political undertakings.

'For God's sake don't talk politics. . . . The only thing that interests me is style', James Joyce once said to his brother Stanislaus.[6] My reading of *Heart of Darkness* has helped me to recognize how indivisible these terms – 'politics' and 'style' – truly are. An element of style so basic that we probably confine it to a point of grammar, not even rhetoric, is the use of 'we'. Next time you read *Heart of*

Darkness, pay particular attention to it. There is a real awkwardness in Marlow's use of pronouns – we/you/I – particularly when he is under stress. (A paradigm case occurs when he is going up-river, pp. 66–9.) If we deconstruct this stylistic turbulence or crux, we have to wonder: who is this 'we'? 'We' implies a familiar, mutually supportive conversing community; who belongs to it? And why does Marlow so insistently resort to the isolating 'I' when he is under pressure? By extension (again the words gesture beyond the text, the figure beyond the canvas) I as a reader need to try to position myself through identification or difference with these pronouns. Where do I stand in this? Or, to give the question its political form, am I 'one of us'? What do 'I' share with this 'we'? And who is this 'I' anyway?

The text confronts me, as a reader, with quite uncomfortable questions. Do I occupy the same contradictory position as my surrogates, the audience on the *Nellie*? In their professional capacities we have seen how, wittingly or unwittingly, they might well be fellow actors in the great colonizing enterprise. Are they, like the knitters, 'sitting at the other end of such an affair'? And if they are, am I? If imperialism by its very nature often works at arm's length (like the doctor at headquarters or the French man-of-war), and if distance and indirection are primary means by which it conceals from itself the true nature of its own activity, then the audience to the tale may also be participants. But – and this is vital in the reception of *Heart of Darkness* and potentially in that of any narrative – they are participants with a difference. They can come to comprehend precisely the fact of their own political position as they receive the story. The act of narration places before them, in distilled and objectified form, a body of experience, including the experience of their own historical complicity, which is thus open for their scrutiny and understanding. I take this as epitomizing the nature and strength of all significant and demanding literature: that it can present contradictions, including those embraced by its audience, and through exposing these enable the recipient to come to some sort of self-knowledge and appraisal. Without necessarily grunting or growling, each reader of *Heart of Darkness* needs to ask if, or rather how, she or he 'sees the story'. Do the same contradictions hold for readers as for Marlow's listeners?

My general point is that even 'minimal' stylistic traits have a political dimension. Not this time as apparent as the explicit politics of colonialism (examined in Chapter 4), nor that involved in the cultural stereotyping of civilization and savagery (Chapters 5 and 6), but rather one we could call the politics of the narrating situation. It's this kind of richness in the text which I find so impressive about Conrad's writing. The novel is so finely 'worked' that its concerns permeate its texture at every level. Issues like the political, say, don't 'just' exist at the explicit level of content or thematic abstraction. They infiltrate every aspect of the fictional construction to include the 'merest' formal, textual detail, such as whether to use 'we' or 'I'. Indeed, these may be just the sort of 'secondary notions' which Conrad spoke of as carrying the meaning of the work.[7]

Surely, you might say, these are details, mere details! How can they do so much work? For that matter, isn't it quite possible that Conrad slipped up now and again, and was unaware of the sliding in the text between the written and the oral, say, or the play of pronouns? True; and to say that the details of the work carry so much weight might suggest authorial control over the text's meaning. Indeed one of the main points which my reading of the work has led me to 'see' (to use Conrad's neat little word) is that the narrative – indeed any language performance – may well reveal more than the user of the language might know or fully control. As my argument about colonial and cultural stereotypes sought to show, there is a powerful sense in which 'language speaks, not men'.[8] Although in one obvious sense the author is the producer of the text – it is after all Conrad who wrote the words, and it is his specific history in all its fullness and contradiction which has gone into its making – we cannot straight-forwardly invoke him as the conscious organizer of the meanings we have found in the work. My discussion of Chinua Achebe's critique in Chapter 4 alluded to some difficulties along this path, not least finding out what the author's intended meaning might be without in turn having recourse to further interpretation. Another difficulty, which the novel's critique of language has helped me recognize, is more immediately pertinent. It is the way language so constantly plays tricks on its users. When we say, 'In Conrad the darkness is never just physical', or something like that, 'Conrad' means the writing of Conrad. It may seem slight, but the metonymic use of the proper name insinuates, or certainly gestures towards, authorial intention. So powerful, I would argue, is the readerly drive to attribute cause and intention that we slip over such figures of speech, and thus reveal unwittingly a certain way of looking. It takes a great deal of critical effort even to become aware of it. I am quite sure that I am guilty of the fault in this book, defending myself only on the grounds that consistency is the refuge of bores.

The example of our ambiguous use of Conrad's name suggests that when we alight on meaningful intention, we may well be discovering our own. This has in fact been one of my arguments. In trying to become more aware of reading processes, I came to recognize how much within the fictional world of *Heart of Darkness* had to do not with 'Things in Themselves' but characters' and their ideologies' reading of things. The perception of things, a particular way of seeing, is always interested, intentional, projective. It is of course possible that I am proving my point by tautology, that I am projecting onto my reading of the book the omnipresence and inescapability of reading. At any rate, a notion involving projection and reading lies at the centre of two very different approaches to literature: the psychological and reader-response theories of the text. It is with these two odd bed-mates that I will conclude.

These arguments, which are being currently much debated, offer in some respects thoroughly antagonistic arguments about literary works and their interpretation. Theories based on psychological processes locate the unconscious self of the writer as the profoundest source and defining ground of the text. The text is then readable as a symptomatic expression of unconscious drives on the part of the writer. Reader-response theories, in an extreme version, proclaim the 'death of the Author', rejecting the Author, understood as the metaphysical concept of an originating principle, a divine sole possessor of an inspired pen. Such theories argue that meaning is something produced by the reader in the act of narrative consumption, not somehow hidden there by the controlling writer. Paradoxically, both views have in common the postulate that at any rate we cannot appeal to the conscious intention of the writer as the arbitrating authority for meaning, which is produced rather by unconscious or readerly projection. Both theories offer alternatives to the question of whether it is necessary to attribute to Conrad an almost God-like power to manage every aspect of detail of style and theme in order to deliver meaning.

An engaging version of the psychological account of textual meaning can be found in the essay by Frederick Crews from which I quoted in Chapter 3. He argues, in summary:

> Conrad's most significant level of discourse is the unconscious level, where inadmissible wishes are entertained, blocked and allowed a choked and guarded expression . . . his engagement in his plots would seem to have more to do with self-exculpation than with dispassionate analysis. . . . He typically diverts our interest from the hero's gloomy mind to his lush surroundings, which are stocked with misplaced energies. . . . *Heart of Darkness* is in the most agitated sense an autobiographical work. Far from criticizing Marlow, Conrad was using him to recapitulate and try to master the Congo experience he himself had sought out and undergone in 1890 – an experience that led not to philosophical conclusions but to a physical and nervous breakdown.[9]

Crews's critical project locates the real meaning of the text in Conrad's unconscious desires and fears. He sees critics who hurry on to the 'moral issues which are taken so very seriously' as evading the deep uneasiness in the work and which the work generates in its readers. He specifically attacks Leavis in this regard for criticizing Conrad's obscuring 'adjectival insistence' without asking what he is trying to hide. (At the same time, Crews remarks, Leavis is banally satisfied with morally praising him as 'a gallant, simple sailor'.)[10] Very cleverly, Crews seeks to outmanoeuvre other critical positions by insinuating bad faith or repression on their part.

I find these arguments stimulating but wrong. Let me put my objections first, for I have difficulties specifically with Crews's arguments and generally with his kind of psychological approach. First, the reading places at an unconscious level aspects of the novel which on my reading are quite clearly conscious – as, for example, the therapeutic value of work. If Marlow explicitly tells his audience that work deflects him from too much self-inquiry or indulgence, suppressing the appeal of his instinct to howl and dance, it is hard to see how this could be unconscious repression on Conrad's part.

There is, in addition, an either/or structure to Crews's argument, which I find reductive. If Conrad's Congo trip and the novel which arose out of it is of psychological interest, it cannot apparently raise any 'philosophical' questions. To push this argument further – it proposes that if we see the novel forested with symbols of private obsession, we cannot simultaneously see the work as engaging with political questions about the destructive forces of economic and military colonialism. If we take the French destroyer's guns as a phallic symbol of impotence, then on Crews's argument, we are diverted from the political.

But its dualistic structure ('the most significant level of discourse is the unconscious level') may be the most problematic aspect of his argument. Interestingly it repeats the powerful model of meaning which Marlow himself at times evokes: 'the surface truth' which covers a reality hiding beneath. As a way of thinking about meaning, it is a very powerful metaphor – and a very flattering one, for it suggests that (1) there is a real meaning, that (2) it is hidden/unconscious, and that (3) I have seen it. Which critic or teacher (I include myself among them!) doesn't earn his or her bread because of a vested interest in this credo? There are, after all, other possible models:

(a) there is a hidden meaning, but no one can find it;
(b) there is a hidden meaning which only certain people can know, and I am not quite one of them;
(c) there might be a hidden meaning, but no one knows if there is;
(d) there is no meaning, hidden or not;
(e) the absence of a meaning is the meaning.

Crews's version drastically reduces the number of potential

variations. According to my reading, I would hazard that *Heart of Darkness* offers (contradictory) evidence for *all* of them.

But there are several things to be said for Crews's approach. We have, after all, learned that we can't take things at face value. We can and should, as I have done, read symptomatically against the grain, teasing out significant trouble. However, the recognition of contradictions – e.g. Marlow on women, or Marlow's semi-colonialism – does not require either a grounding outside the text in Conrad's psyche, nor an origin in one primal source of contradiction. But that said, although in his critique of other critics he runs the risk of seeing moral issues as superficial evasions, he does at least identify readers' vested interests in the readings they make. This has been one of my points, even if I do not agree with Crews on the implied priorities.

Against this view of locating the originating meaning in the author, let us now set reader-response theories, very current in critical discourse. The term 'reader-response' is a broad designation for several and differing critical arguments concerned with the reader's relation to the text in establishing textual meaning. The brilliant French critic Roland Barthes is one of the most exciting (if maverick) proponents of this position.

> We know now that a text is not a line of words releasing a single 'theological' meaning (the 'message' of the Author-God) but a multi-dimensional space in which a variety of writings, none of them original, blend and clash. . . . Once the Author is removed, the claim to decipher a text becomes quite futile. To give a text an Author is to impose a limit on that text, to furnish it with a final signified, to close the writing . . . a text is made of multiple writings, drawn from many cultures and entering into mutual relations of dialogues, parody, contestation, but there is one place where this multiplicity is focused and that place is the reader, not, as was hitherto said, the author. The reader is the space on which all the quotations that make up a writing are inscribed without any of them being lost; a text's unity lies not in its origin but in its destination. Yet this destination cannot any longer be personal: the reader is without history, biography, psychology; he is simply that someone who holds together in a single field all the traces by which the written text is constituted.[11]

I do not wish to imply that the passage above is 'typical' of theorists concerned with the reader's involvement with meaning, in that such critics are more notable for their diverse opinions than their group spirit. But Barthes's writings have been extremely influential in opening up this area to critical speculation, perhaps because they are colourful, witty, and controversial. Indeed, Barthes has a habit of casting intellectual Molotov cocktails into academic senior common rooms and slipping off before the explosion to watch the debris fall. So we ought to read his playful rhetoric against the grain, too. When he talks of the death of the Author, he is not announcing the disconcerting and somewhat premature demise of those who are still with us. It is not actual historical figures he is talking of, but rather the assumed power they possess in our imaginations. His basic position is to argue that we have attended too much to the idea of the Author as originating meaning. The metaphysic (as he would see it) of Authority should be subverted. After all, works talk more than the author can consciously know or control. Paradoxically, on one level, Crews would agree with this. For him, Conrad is not consciously controlling his effects, or mastering his meanings either. But the comparison ends there. For Crews, any philosophical, moral, political or mythological readings need translating into the primal discourse of the psyche. For Barthes, all of these exist as adjacent codes of discourse activated by the reader, through which the text can be played.

For Barthes, meanings reside in the reading, produced by the free play of the readerly mind unconstrained by the oppressive idea of a dominant presence of the Author God (or the Author Analysand). Individual readers, liberated from their own historical and social positions at the moment of literary absorption, can remake themselves while remaking the book, inscribing the work and themselves with new possibilities of significance. Rather than contesting this view head on, I would suggest that the deliberately provoking formulation of this position is Barthes's playful and dialectical way (he learnt a lot from Brecht) of freeing readers into defining for themselves their own positions (not passively incorporating others' positioning of them), not outside history but consciously inserted within it. But it is precisely such elemental terms as history, society, psychology, civilization, which *Heart of Darkness* has radically questioned, too.

I suppose the final value of such criticism – indeed, any critical writing – lies in the interest it provokes. The danger is that the critic first conceals, then searches out, what is not worth finding. Or chases the obvious with the indefatigable enthusiasm of a short-sighted detective. Barthes runs no such dangers.

Nor does the critical thinking I believe Conrad's writing encourages. It discloses the crucial importance of taking nothing for granted – including a passing remark of Marlow's. 'If we may believe what we read', he says at one point, talking of stories about the Romans (p. 30). To transform this from an easy cliché and reread it as a critical, political practice for ourselves, we need to gloss it: 'What is it that I need to believe, or am prepared to believe, to believe what I read?' It is this task, to become aware of my readerly assumptions, which *Heart of Darkness* constantly challenges me to and which I hope this Guide has opened up for you.

Notes

Chapter 1: Meanings and Readings (pages 1–10)

1 Franz Kafka, 'The leopard in the temple', *Paradoxes and Parables*, (Schocken Books, 1961), p. 93.

2 By Modernist I am referring to that movement within European culture, dating roughly from 1880 to 1930, which saw itself as responding in a particularly self-conscious and radical way to what it regarded as a crisis of belief in societal values and art's own status within the community. Neither programmatic nor uniform, Modernism is nevertheless a useful term to describe a general tendency marked by a critical artistic self-scrutiny, a rejection of inherited conventions of representation, and a variously enthusiastic or sceptical renunciation of any stable notion of truth concerning identity, history, knowledge and value. Useful introductions to the area can be found in Faulkner, *Modernism* (Methuen, 1977), and Bradbury and McFarlane, *Modernism* (Penguin, 1976).

3 Conrad, cited in A. Symons, *Notes on Joseph Conrad: With Some Unpublished Letters* (Arthur Symons and Myers & Co., 1925), p. 18.

4 Ed. Z. Najder, *Conrad's Polish Background* (Oxford University Press, 1964), p. 239.

5 Letter to Ramsay MacDonald, 27 May 1924, cited in Z. Najder, *Joseph Conrad, A Chronicle* (Rutgers University Press, 1983), p. 488.

6 Norman Sherry, *Conrad's Western World* (Cambridge University Press, 1971) and *Conrad's Eastern World* (Cambridge University Press, 1966), provide an invaluable resource for a knowledge of Conrad's experiences and their relationship to his writing.

7 J. Conrad, *Congo Diary*, ed. Z. Najder (Doubleday & Co., 1978), p. 8.

Chapter 2: Stories and Histories (pages 11–23)

1 Recent literary theory has sought to articulate the nature of this active readerly function in some detail. Roland Barthes, particularly in *S/Z* (Hill and Wang, 1974) and *The Pleasure of the Text* (Hill and Wang, 1975), and Umberto Eco in *The Role of the Reader* (Hutchinson, 1981) propose that meaning does not reside autonomously within the work, simply to be passively 'consumed' by the reader, but that the reader positively constitutes the text in its fullness. But – and here's the give and take – even as the reader constitutes the text, he or she is also presupposed by it. It both assumes and to a degree creates an 'implied reader' who brings into play the (ideologically laden) codes and conventions within which the work exists. (As individual readers, we, with our own experiences and social and cultural determinations, are not in any particular instance identical with this implied model reader.) Mikhail

Bakhtin, *The Dialogic Imagination* (University of Texas, 1981), argues that novels are constituted by a number of mixed discourses, which liberate the reader into engaging with a fuller 'polysemous' play of meanings. In all three theories the activity of reading to produce meanings is paramount.

2 Conrad to R. Cunninghame Graham, 8 February 1899, in *Collected Letters* (Cambridge University Press, 1986), Vol. 2, 1898–1902, pp. 157–8.

3 *Middlemarch* (Penguin, 1965), p. 111.

Chapter 3: Senses of Place (pages 23–36)

1 For Conrad's own youthful enthusiasm, see *A Personal Record* (1912; rpt. Dent, 1975), p. 13.

2 See Sherry, *Conrad's Western World*.

3 Conrad to Curle, 24 April 1922, in R. Curle, *Conrad to a Friend* (Doubleday, NY, 1928), p. 112.

4 Frederick Crews, 'Conrad's uneasiness – and ours', in *Out of My System* (Oxford University Press, 1975), pp. 56–7.

5 Albert Guerard, *Conrad the Novelist* (Harvard University Press, 1958), p. 38.

6 Lillian Feder, 'Marlow's descent into hell', in *Nineteenth Century Fiction*, IX (March 1955), pp. 280–92 (reprinted in ed. R. W. Stallman, *The Art of Joseph Conrad* (Michigan State University Press, 1960), pp. 162–70), detects in *Heart of Darkness* not only literary echoes but a virtual reworking of Aeneas' visit to Hades in Book Six of Virgil's *Aeneid*. In Evans' account (below) we venture into another darkness, Dante's.

7 R. O. Evans, 'Conrad's underworld', *Modern Fiction Studies*, II (May 1956), pp. 56–62. Reprinted in ed. R. W. Stallman, *op.cit.*, pp. 171–81.

8 Here, in brief, are some of my responses: (1) reductive, (2) inaccurate, (3) insensitive to the problematic tone, (4) silly. At times all self-respecting critics embrace one or more of these qualities in combination; but to embrace all four simultaneously and programmatically seems to be courting danger. I say 'programmatically' because it seems to me that to allegorize *Heart of Darkness* into a work 'patterned after that of the Inferno' is to try (and I think fail) to impose on it a fixity of relations which (1) ignores the very different ideological sensibilities of the writers and their specific cultural and historical positions; (2) mythologizes away the economic and political barbarities imposed on colonized Africa; (3) reduces down to an unambiguous 'clear moral insight' (which incidentally is never elaborated on) the moral and political complexities, contradictions, and equivocations of the work. Now you may wish to read the Evans' essay in full to see if I have over-simplified his reading and been unduly (1) reductive, (2) inaccurate, (3) insensitive, and/or (4) silly.

9 Najder, *Conrad's Polish Background*, p. 74.

10 For an interesting letter on the Absurd which mixes the profoundly pessimistic with the practical, see Conrad's letter to R. Cunninghame Graham, 14 December 1897, in *Collected Letters*, Vol. 1, p. 423.

Would you seriously wish to tell such a man: 'Know thyself'?

Understand that thou art nothing, less than a shadow, more insignificant than a drop of water in the ocean, more fleeting than the illusion of a dream. Would you?

But I hear the postman. Au revoir till next week.

For comparable important letters in the metaphysical vein, see *Collected Letters*, Vol. 2, pp. 17, 30, which talk meaningfully of a meaningless universe.

Chapter 4: Colonialism; Semi-colonialism (pages 37–58)

1 This comes in an article in the 20 January 1891 edition of *Petit Journal*, a mass-circulating French newspaper; it describes government troops fighting in the Western Sudan. Cited in William Schneider, *An Empire for the Masses; The French Popular Image of Africa, 1870–1900* (Greenwood Press, Westport, Connecticut, 1982), p. 72.

2 As so often, Bob Dylan provides pertinent lyrics; this from 'Sweetheart Like You' on *Infidels* (CBS, 1983).

3 From the works of, for example, John Hobson, *Imperialism: A Study* (1902) and Lenin, *Imperialism* (1916), onwards, competing theories have been advanced for the causes and specific forms of this imperialist endeavour. Some theories emphasize the economic: the need for raw materials and expanding markets, and for areas allowing for the more profitable investment of surplus capital. Others stress the political: the need to create and mobilize a sense of national identity, as in the case of Bismarck's Germany, recently united in 1871; to protect trade routes to older British colonies in India and the Far East; and to 'export from Europe' the tensions and conflicts created by the in-fighting of the European powers. Clearly, these causes of imperialism are not mutually exclusive, and the forms colonization took varied according to the dominance of one or another of them. What they shared was the development, to a greater or lesser degree, of a military, administrative, financial, and communications network in Africa. This colonial infra-structure, paid for through private or state intervention, was necessary for the establishment and exploitation of European economic and political interests.

4 King Leopold II of Belgium, 1898. Cited in the Norton Critical Edition of *Heart of Darkness*, ed. R. Kimbrough (Norton, 1988), p. 79. In addition to detailed editorial apparatus, this edition has a very useful collection of secondary material, including critical essays.

5 E. D. Morel, *King Leopold's Rule in Africa* (William Heinemann, 1904). Morel had been campaigning for several years about 'The Congo Scandal' and in 1903 established The Congo Reform Society with Conrad's friend Roger Casement. See Ruth Slade, *King Leopold's Congo* (Oxford University Press, 1962) and L. Gann and P. Duigan, *The Rulers of Belgian Africa, 1884–1914* (Princeton University Press, 1979) for a fuller account.

6 Cited in Slade, *op. cit.*, p. 175.

7 See Sherry, *Conrad's Western World*, pp. 92–118, and Ian Watt, *Conrad in the Nineteenth Century* (University of California Press, 1979), pp. 141–6.

8 Slade, *ibid*.

9 *Collected Letters*, Vol. 2, pp. 139–40.

10 'Geography and some explorers', in *Last Essays*, ed. R. Curle (Dent, 1926), p. 17.

11 Cited in Najder, *Conrad's Polish Background*, p. 242.

12 For a version of the first position, see Cedric Watts, *Conrad's Heart of Darkness* (Mursia International, Milan, 1977), pp. 73–4; for the second see F. R. Leavis's account in *The Great Tradition* (1948; Penguin, 1972), pp. 196–7.

13 Brecht, *Poems 1913–1956* (Eyre Methuen, 1981), p. 252.

14 Chinua Achebe, 'An image of Africa', in *The Massachusetts Review*, 18:4, pp. 782–94 (Winter, 1977), p. 788. See also Achebe's critique in 'Viewpoint' (TLS No. 4010, 1 February 1980) and his own novel, *Things Fall Apart* (Heinemann, 1968), a sort of Heart of Darkness from the African end.

15 Conrad's *Congo Diary* and letters of 1890 reveal how he felt initially that he was the object of the Société Anonyme's disregard and exploitation, as well as being a potential agent of it. This personally located anger might well be at the root of the tone of justifiable protest which pervades the pages of the novel.

16 For critical accounts on this controversy see, apart from Achebe's powerful attack, Cedric Watts' eloquent and measured defence of Conrad's position in '"A Bloody Racist": About Achebe's View of Conrad,' in *Yearbook of English Studies*, 13 (1983), pp. 196–209. Patrick Brantlinger, '*Heart of Darkness*: Anti-Imperialism, Racism, or Impressionism?', *Criticism*, 27 (1985), pp. 363–85, offers a helpful survey of recent argument.

17 Conrad, 'Author's note' (1920) to *The Secret Agent* (Penguin, 1985), pp. 39, 41.

18 Achebe, *op. cit.*, p. 785.

19 Achebe, *op. cit.*, p. 787.

20 F. R. Leavis, *The Great Tradition*, (1948; Penguin, 1972), p. 211.

21 Conrad to Aniela Zagórska and to Cunninghame Graham, *Collected Letters*, Vol. 2, pp. 230 and 207 respectively.

22 See for example his letters of 23 January, 1898, and 8 February, 1899, in *Collected Letters*, Vol. 2, pp. 24–5, 157–61, which powerfully express anti-socialist sentiments, critical of the democratic idealism Cunninghame Graham embraced.

23 Walter Benjamin, 'Theses on the philosophy of history', *Illuminations* (Fontana, 1973), p. 258.

Chapter 5: 'Civilization' and 'Savagery': Marlow Imagining the Other (pages 59–85)

1 Franz Kafka, *The Castle* (Penguin, 1957), p. 42.

2 N. Sherry, *Conrad's Western World*, p. 61.

3 Z. Najder, *Joseph Conrad, A Chronicle*, pp. 135–6.

4 J. Conrad, *Congo Diary*, pp. 34–5.

5 J. Conrad, 'Geography and some explorers', in *Last Essays*, p. 17.

6 In its broadest sense, hermeneutics concerns the theory of interpretation, and the problem of what determines the meaning of a text. Ancient in its (sacred scriptural) origins, its most important contemporary (secular) development is found in the work of the German philosopher Hans-Georg Gadamer. My present use of the term invokes its more limited

application found particularly in Roland Barthes, *S/Z*. Barthes proposes 'hermeneutic' to describe the narrative structure of enigma – of questions posed (what does it mean? who did it?) which excite in the reader a desire for a (characteristically delayed) answer. See *S/Z*, pp. 19, 84–6.

7 F. R. Leavis, *The Great Tradition*, pp. 204–5, 207.

8 P. O'Prey, Introduction, *Heart of Darkness* (Penguin, 1983), p. 22.

9 O. Wilde, 'The Decay of Lying', in *De Profundis and Other Writings* (Penguin, 1984), p. 67.

10 The myth of cannibalism is particularly potent and resistant to rational inquiry. A recent anthropological study by W. Arens, *The Man-Eating Myth* (Oxford University Press, 1979), brilliantly argues that despite the massive amount of literature on or alluding to cannibalism, there is no satisfactory first-hand account of it as a socially approved custom, ritually practised anywhere in the world. But critics (and novelists) still find it good copy. Sherry talks confidently of Conrad's black crew being cheerful Bangala cannibals (Sherry, pp. 59–60). He perpetuates this fiction to 'confirm' the 'accuracy' of Conrad's fictional rendering.

An interesting gloss on this comes in H. H. Johnston's *The River Congo* (Sampson Low & Co., 1895), published five years after Conrad's trip:

> Merely because of the abundance of human remains in this village many would jump to the conclusion of cannibalism. [But . . .] I asked some of them confidentially if they ever eat man, proffering the inquiry with assumed carelessness, so that if they might feel any false shame in admitting this addition to their diet they would be reassured by my freedom from prejudice and confess. At first however they did not clearly understand me, but when . . . I had made my meaning plainer, they repelled the suggestion with the utmost horror, replying . . . an emphatic ('No, no, no') 'Vê, vê, vê', then adding a timid inquiry, 'No Baïo?' ('And you? Do you?') (pp. 180–1)

Johnston also has graphic descriptions (p. 115) of huge logs, carved and painted as human heads, surrounding many habitations. A possible, albeit less chilling, explanation for Kurtz's heads? Conrad's disturbing tale, 'Falk: A Reminiscence' (Heinemann, 1903), returns to the theme of cannibalism, though this time the activity is restricted to Europeans.

11 On the image of Africa and Africans, there exists a very extensive literature. Much of this seeks to trace both the literary origins and the ideological functions of European ideas on the African as 'noble savage', 'barbarian', 'primitive'. A seminal work and useful starting point for further reading would be Philip Curtin, *The Image of Africa: British Ideas and Action 1780–1850* (University of Wisconsin Press, 1963). Also H. A. C. Cairns, *Prelude to Imperialism: British Reactions to Central African Society, 1840–1890* (Routledge & Kegan Paul, 1965) and Brian V. Street, *The Savage in Literature: Representations of 'Primitive' Society in English Fiction, 1858–1920* (Routledge & Kegan Paul, 1975), are very helpful.

12 H. Spencer, 'The Primitive Man-Intellectual', in *The Principles of Sociology* (1876; Williams and Norgate, 1893), Vol. I, p. 89.

13 C. Darwin, *The Descent of Man and Selection in Relation to Sex* (rev. ed., 1874; John Murray, 1901), p. 946.

14 Fothergill, see p. 62 above.
15 This recalls the story of the party bore. 'But, I've talked quite long enough about myself. Now tell me, what do *you* think of me?'

Chapter 6: Endings: Crying, Dying, Lying . . . and Telling Stories (pages 85–113)

1 Conrad, 'Cookery', *Last Essays* (Dent, 1926), p. 217.
2 Watt, *op. cit.*, p. 245.
3 Walter Benjamin, *op. cit.*, p. 94.
4 Lionel Trilling, *Beyond Culture* (Penguin, 1967), pp. 32–3.
5 Jacques Berthoud, *Joseph Conrad: The Major Phase* (Cambridge University Press, 1978), pp. 60–1.
6 Douglas Brown, 'From Heart of Darkness to Nostromo: an approach to Conrad', *The Modern Age: The Pelican Guide to English Literature*, Vol. 7, ed. Boris Ford (Penguin, 1973), p. 145.
7 Ian Watt, *op. cit.*, pp. 236, 238.
8 E. M. Forster, 'Joseph Conrad: A Note', *Abinger Harvest* (Penguin, 1967), p. 152.
9 S. Freud, *Civilization and Its Discontents*, Penguin Freud Library, Vol. 12 (Penguin, 1985), p. 268.
10 Conrad, *Notes on Life & Letters* (Dent, 1921), p. 13.
11 Jessie Conrad's letter to Meldrum, 6 February, 1910, *Conrad's Letters to William Blackwood and David Meldrum*, ed. William Blackburn (Duke University Press, 1958), p. 192.
12 *The Nigger of the 'Narcissus'* (Oxford University Press, 1984), p. xlii.

Chapter 7: In Lieu of Concluding . . . (pages 114–123)

1 Cf. Theodor Adorno, *Aesthetic Theory* (Routledge & Kegan Paul, 1984), p. 1; my translation from the 1970 German edition.
2 See above, Chapter 6, p. 113.
3 Conrad, 'A Familiar Preface', *A Personal Record*, p. xi.
4 For a fuller account of 'deconstruction', particularly its concern for language and meaning, see Jeremy Tambling's Open Guide, *What Is Literary Language?* (Open University Press, 1988).
5 See for example Fredric Jameson, *The Political Unconscious* (Methuen, 1981), pp. 206–80, which proposes that 'a case could be made for reading Conrad not as an early modernist, but rather an anticipation of that later and quite different thing . . . post-modernism' (p. 219).
6 Cited in Richard Ellmann, *James Joyce* (Oxford University Press, 1965), p. 710.
7 See above, Chapter 2, pp. 17–18.
8 That 'language speaks, not men' is a polemical reduction of the view, powerfully formulated by Heidegger and later taken up by some feminist/post-structuralist thinkers, that we need to re-think our 'natural' idea that the speaker of a language is the controlling subject manipulating language to her or his own prior needs and thoughts. See 'Language' in Martin Heidegger, *Poetry, Language, Thought* (Harper & Row, 1971).
9 Frederick Crews, *op. cit.*, pp. 46, 50, 58.
10 For Leavis, see above, Chapter 4, p. 53.
11 Barthes, 'Death of the Author,' *Image: Music: Text*, ed. Stephen Heath (Fontana, 1977), pp. 146–8.

Suggestions for Further Reading

Some of the most incisive commentary on specific modernist works is offered by other such writing. Here, theory is indivisible from practice. It is not surprising that Conrad himself supplies us with some of the best intertextual 'criticism' on *Heart of Darkness* by way of his other works. Those featuring Marlow as central narrator/protagonist are particularly pertinent: *Youth* (1898) and *Lord Jim* (1900). (See also *Chance* (1913).) *Nostromo* (1904) further articulates the politics of imperialism, via a characteristically complex narrative structure. It provides a powerful comparison of the idealizing habits of 'civilizing' men . . . and their idealistic women. The portrayal of major female protagonists can be traced in *The Secret Agent* (1907) and *Under Western Eyes* (1911). In the former, Winnie Verloc declares that 'things do not stand much looking into.' It's a sentiment glossing Marlow's apprehension of 'the surface truth' of things; and also confirming a certain sort of (male) perception and representation of women. *Under Western Eyes* also pursues to a profound political and psychological level the argument that what is taken for the Real is a matter of reading and interpretation. As the narrator tendentiously puts it, 'a man's real life is that accorded to him in the thoughts of other men'. Finally, *Victory* (1915) takes up the themes of moral scepticism and 'civilization' and its discontents.

For biographical information, consult Conrad's *Collected Letters*, ed. Frederick Karl. Volume 1 (1861–97) and Volume 2 (1898–1902) cover the crucial period for *Heart of Darkness*. Other important collections are G. Jean-Aubry, *Joseph Conrad: Life and Letters*, Vols. 1 & 2 (Heinemann, 1927); *Letters from Conrad*, 1895 to 1924, ed. Edward Garnett (Nonesuch, 1928); *Joseph Conrad's Letters to R. B. Cunninghame Graham*, ed. Cedric Watts (Cambridge University Press, 1969); and *Conrad's Polish Background*, ed. Z. Najder (Oxford University Press, 1964). The last two works, apart from their fascinating content, have particularly interesting editorial material. Since the early standard critical biography, Jocelyn Baines's *Joseph Conrad* (1960; Penguin, 1971), there have appeared Z. Najder's and Frederick Karl's major biographies, which together with Ian Watt's *Conrad in the Nineteenth Century*, are comparable to Norman Sherry's work as essential resources. For a psychoanalytical biography, see Bernard Meyer, *Joseph Conrad* (Princeton University Press, 1967).

Critical works on Conrad are legion. The primary bibliography, Teets and Gerber, *Joseph Conrad: An Annotated Bibliography of Writings about Him* (Illinois University Press, 1971), extends from 1895 to 1966; more recent surveys can be found in *Conradiana* (Texas Tech University), a quarterly journal devoted to Conrad studies. My suggestions, necessarily selective, mainly centre on some of the thematic tracks this *Guide* has traced but won't include works cited in the endnotes, which you should consult for further guidance.

For the historical and colonial aspects of the novel see Hunt Hawkins, 'Conrad's Critique of Imperialism in Heart of Darkness', *PMLA*, 94, no. 2 (1979), and Jonah Raskin, 'Imperialism: Conrad's Heart of Darkness', *Journal of Contemporary History*, 2, No. 2 (1967), who sees it as a radical critique of imperialist decadence. Benita Parry, *Conrad and Imperialism* (Macmillan, 1983), develops the ideological emphasis in this interpretation, analysing Conrad's ambivalence to the imperialist ideology which underpinned contemporary colonial activity.

On Conrad's representation of 'the savage', see, apart from Achebe, K. K. Ruthven, 'The Savage God: Conrad and Lawrence', *The Critical Quarterly*, x, Nos. 1 and 2 (1968), which endorses European constructions of the 'primitive' as representing the pre-civilized 'whole man'; and M. M. Mahood, *The Colonial Encounter: A Reading of Six Novels* (Rex Collings, 1977). For Conrad's links with Darwinism, see Allan Hunter, *Joseph Conrad and the Ethics of Darwinism* (Croom Helm, 1983). Indispensable for a theoretical account of the issues of cross-cultural representation is Edward Said, *Orientalism* (Routledge & Kegan Paul, 1978).

Jeremy Hawthorn, *Joseph Conrad: Language and Fictional Self-Consciousness* (Arnold, 1979), is a stimulating general account from within a Marxist perspective of five major works, linking questions of fictionality to political practice. Aaron Fogel, *Coercion to Speak: Conrad's Poetics of Dialogue* (Harvard University Press, 1985), applies theories of discourse from Bakhtin and post-structuralist writing to Conrad's works. A challenging chapter in Peter Brooks' *Reading for the Plot* (Random House, 1984), combines questions about discourse and utterance with those concerning the narrative structure of the novel. Narratological issues also surface in Cedric Watts, *The Deceptive Text* (Harvester, 1984). *Conrad Revisited* (University of Alabama Press, 1985), ed. Ross Murfin, collects among others two important contributions – a post-structuralist account by J. Hillis Miller, arguing for the work as an 'apocalyptic' text without revelation; and an essay by Bruce Johnson, relocating Conrad's 'impressionism' in a broader philosophical context. But though Murfin proclaims 'Conrad for the 80's', neither he nor others have taken feminist theory significantly into account. This in some measure I have tried to remedy. The lack is interesting, for in other respects the history of Conrad criticism can be read as a record in miniature of the cultural history of twentieth century critical thinking – a course admirably charted by Terry Eagleton, *Literary Theory* (Blackwell, 1983), and David Lodge, *Modern Criticism and Theory: A Reader* (Longman, 1988). Perhaps the absence is part of that history too.

Index